# 50

# Shared texts

## Photocopiable texts for shared reading

Fiction, non-fiction and poetry ●

Annotated versions ●

Discussion prompts ●

Nikki Gamble

# Credits

**Author**
Nikki Gamble

**Illustrations**
Terry Burton

**Series Consultants**
Fiona Collins and
Alison Kelly

**Series Designer**
Anna Oliwa

**Editor**
Roanne Charles

**Designer**
Anna Oliwa

**Assistant Editor**
Clare Gallaher

Text © 2004 Nikki Gamble
**© 2004 Scholastic Ltd**

Designed using Adobe InDesign

Published by Scholastic Ltd
Villiers House
Clarendon Avenue
Leamington Spa
Warwickshire CV32 5PR

www.scholastic.co.uk

Printed by Bell and Bain Ltd, Glasgow

5 6 7 8 9   7 8 9 0 1 2 3

**British Library Cataloguing-in-Publication Data**
A catalogue record for this book is available from the British Library.

**ISBN 0-439-98478-5**
**ISBN 978-0439-98478-2**

# Contents

 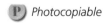

N *Teacher's notes*     P *Photocopiable*

# Term 2 *continued*

# Term 3

**N** *Teacher's notes*     **P** *Photocopiable*

# Introduction

In *50 Shared texts* you will find a range of texts for use in shared reading. In recent years shared text work has become the focal point of daily literacy work, and the success of such shared work is clearly linked to the quality and choice of text. Better understanding of children's reading and writing development has led to the realisation that a greater range of text types, or genres, is needed to enrich children's literacy development. For the busy classroom teacher, seeking out such a range of quality texts can be too time-consuming, which is why appropriate texts have been provided in this book.

## Shared reading

Shared reading is at the heart of the activities in this book and is a cornerstone of the National Literacy Strategy, which states that through shared reading children *begin to recognise important characteristics of a variety of written texts, often linked to style and voice.*

First developed in New Zealand by Don Holdaway, shared reading has been a significant literacy routine for children since the 1980s. Holdaway's research and pioneering work in schools brought the benefits of sharing enlarged texts or Big Books to teachers' attention. From his observations of very young children attending to bedtime stories on a one-to-one basis he realised that a similar intimacy with print could be offered through sharing an enlarged text with a group or class of children. He showed how engagement with Big Books can teach children about the characteristics of different text types, their organisation and distinguishing features, as well as the finer details of print. For example, depending on the teacher's focus, an enlarged recipe could be used at text level to model the way a piece of instructional writing is structured, at sentence level to look at the use of imperative verbs or at word level to focus on a particular phoneme. In relation to literature, the meaning of a poem can be explored at text level, the poet's choice of verbs at sentence level and the rhyming pattern at word level. So, shared reading not only encourages the class to share the actual reading aloud of a text but also enables the teacher to discuss certain language features and support the children in both comprehending and responding to the text.

With younger children, shared reading involves following the text with a pointer to highlight key early concepts of print such as directionality and one-to-one correspondence. With such concepts securely in place, a rather different technique is needed for older children where the focus shifts more to understanding and responding to the text as well as discussing vocabulary and linguistic features. For all children, often the talk surrounding the reading is as important as the reading itself.

Finding the right quality texts for shared reading that will engage and interest the children, as well as meeting the many NLS objectives, can be a difficult task. Once a text is found, you need to identify salient features at word, sentence and text level.

Shared reading is also the springboard for shared writing, guided reading/writing and independent work. Both guided reading and writing provide opportunities for you to guide, support, model and comment on children's response to a text. Activities may involve reading aloud, role-play, performance or writing for a particular purpose. Independent activities may mirror these but need to be clearly structured to enable the children to work independently.

## About this book

The texts in this book are organised term by term, following the NLS framework, so there are examples of fiction, poetry, plays and non-fiction.

For each text, both a blank and annotated version are provided. The former is for use with children and can either be enlarged or projected on an overhead projector; the latter is for teacher information and identifies the features of the text and links with NLS objectives.

## Background

Background information is provided for each text. This will contextualise the extract, fill in any necessary details and give facts about its author as relevant. Information on themes, technical features or other related texts might also feature here.

## Shared reading and discussing the text

This section offers guidance on ways of managing discussion around the text, as well as ways of organising the shared reading. Depending on the age of the children, and demands of the text, different strategies for working with the whole class on the text are given, as well as ways of triggering the children's responses. These include structured discussion suggestions, ideas for role-play, and performance techniques.

## Activities

Building on the reading and discussion, this section suggests activities for both whole-class work and guided or independent group work. There are ideas for further textual analysis, sometimes involving shared writing. As in the previous section, talk is pivotal in developing the children's understanding.

## Extension/further reading

Suggestions for taking activities into a broader context and ideas for linked reading are also provided, where appropriate. Reading may include books of the same genre, or texts that share the theme or the same author.

## The texts

The choice of texts has been driven by the need to ensure that these are quality texts both in content and language. It is hoped that among the selection you will find a mixture of authors and texts, both familiar and new. Whole texts have been provided as far as possible so that children have the satisfaction of reading and appreciating a coherent and complete piece of writing.

Longer texts, such as novels, also need to feature in older children's reading, and sometimes more than one extract from the same carefully chosen novel has been included. Bearing in mind that children should experience as much of the novel as they can, it is recommended that you use the background notes to fill the children in on plot detail, and that you read the story to them or have copies, including a taped version, available for their own reading or listening. Other slots in the curriculum can be used for such reading: private reading, homework, independent group work or story time.

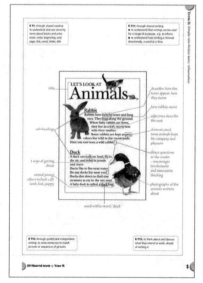

# Range and objectives

## Year R Term 1

| Range | Text | NLS references |
|---|---|---|
| Traditional stories with predictable structures and patterned language | **'The three little pigs'** (extract 1) by Nikki Gamble | W2, W6, T3, T5, T8, T12 |
| | **'The three little pigs'** (extract 2) by Nikki Gamble | W2, S2, T1, T7, T9, T10 |
| | **'In the dark, dark town'** (Traditional) | W4, W6, T6, T9, T10 |
| Modern stories with predictable structures and patterned language | **'Grumble-Rumble!'** (extracts 1 and 2) from *Grumble-Rumble!* by Siobhan Dodds (Dorling Kindersley) | W7, S3, T8, T9, T14 |
| Modern rhymes with predictable structures and patterned language | **'I Like Me!'** by Babs Bell Hajdusiewicz from *My Family and Me* chosen by John Foster (Oxford University Press) | W1, W6, T10, T12 |
| Action verses | **'Painting'** from *One Blue Boat* by Linda Hammond (Puffin) | W11, T8, T10 |
| | **'Goldilocks and the three bears'** by Carolyn Sherwin Bailey from *Oranges & Lemons* compiled by Karen King (Oxford University Press) | W1, W6, T10 |
| Poetry with predictable structures and patterned language | **'Sounds Good'** from *Higgledy-Humbug* by Judith Nicholls (Nelson Thornes) | W2, W4, T14 |
| | **'Bedtime'** by Eleanor Farjeon from *My Family and Me* chosen by John Foster (Oxford University Press) | W1, W8, S4, T12 |
| | **'My Bed'** by Tony Mitton from *A Tiny Teddy* chosen by John Foster (Oxford University Press) | W1, W6, S2, T3, T14 |
| Simple non-fiction texts | **'Party invitation'** by Nikki Gamble | W6, W8, S4, T1, T12, T15 |
| | **'Menu'** by Nikki Gamble | W5, W11, T1, T12, T13, T15 |
| | **'Cooking rules'** by Nikki Gamble | W10, T1, T11 |
| | **'Chocolate apples'** from *Get Set Go! Fruit* by Judy Bastyra (Franklin Watts) | T1, T12, T15 |
| | **'Let's Look at Fruit'** from *Let's Look at Fruit* (Lorenz Books) | W3, W11, T12 |
| | **'My body'** by Nikki Gamble | W5, W11, T1, T12, T15 |

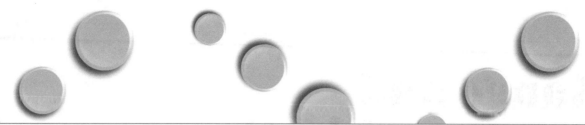

# Year R Term 2

| Range | Text | NLS references |
|---|---|---|
| Stories with patterned language | **'Wet World'** (extracts 1 and 2) from *Wet World* by Norma Simon (Walker Books) | W2, W4, W9, W11, T12 |
| Stories with predictable structures and patterned language | **'A Summery Saturday Morning'** from *A Summery Saturday Morning* by Margaret Mahy (Penguin Books) | W1, W9, T2, T8 |
| | **'Five Ducks Five'** from *Nine Ducks Nine* by Sarah Hayes (Walker Books) | W1, W11, T7, T9, T10 |
| Stories with predictable structures; recounts | **'Wolf's diary'** by Nikki Gamble | W5, T1, T11, T12, T15 |
| Nursery rhymes; action verses | **'I hear thunder'** from *Round and Round the Garden* by Sarah Williams (Oxford University Press) | W5, T6, T7, T10 |
| Poetry with patterned language | **'I Do Not Mind You, Winter Wind'** from *A Cup of Starshine* selected by Jill Bennett (Walker Books) | W1, W4, W10, S3, T3, T11 |
| Modern rhymes | **'The Bad Day ABC'** from *The Bad Day ABC* by Hilda Offen (Puffin) | W2, W3, W4, S3, S4, T10 |
| Poetry with predictable structures | **'A Week at Gran's'** by John Foster from *Around the Year* compiled by John Foster (Oxford University Press) | W2, W4, W5, W6, W9, T6 |
| Modern rhymes | **'Monsters'** from *One Blue Boat* by Linda Hammond (Puffin) | W1, W5, T6, T10 |
| Humorous poetry | **'Cats'** from *Morning Has Broken* by Eleanor Farjeon (Eedermans) | W4, W6, W10, S3, T7, T11 |
| Poetry with predictable structures | **'What's in the Box?'** by Trevor Millum from *A Teeny Tiny Teddy* chosen by John Foster (Oxford University Press) | W1, W2, W4, T12, T15 |
| Poetry with predictable structures and patterned language | **'The Apple and the Worm'** by Robert Heidbreder from *A Cup of Starshine* selected by Jill Bennett (Walker Books) | W5, W10, T7, T12, T14 |
| | **'Here is the Seed'** by John Foster from *Around the Year* compiled by John Foster (Oxford University Press) | W1, T11, T12, T14 |
| Simple non-fiction texts | **'Let's Look at Animals'** from *Let's Look at Animals* by Nicola Tuxworth (Lorenz Books) | T1, T11, T12, T13 |
| | **'Why do sunflowers face the sun?'** from *Why do sunflowers face the sun?* by Terry Martin (Dorling Kindersley) | S1, T1, T3, T11, T12 |
| | **'Children's Collection'** seed packet from Thompson & Morgan Ltd | W5, T1, T12, T15 |
| | **'Weather map'** by Nikki Gamble | W10, T1, T11, T15 |

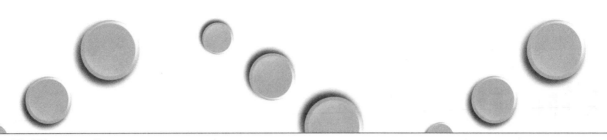

# Year R Term 3

| Range | Text | NLS references |
|---|---|---|
| Traditional stories with predictable structures and patterned language | **'The Three Billy Goats Gruff'** (extract 1) by Nikki Gamble | W2, S2, T5, T7, T8 |
| | **'The Three Billy Goats Gruff'** (extract 2) by Nikki Gamble | T5, T7, T8, T9, T13 |
| | **'Chicken Licken'** (extract 1) from *The Puffin Book of Five-Minute Animal Stories* (Puffin) | S1, S2, T5, T7, T12 |
| | **'Chicken Licken'** (extract 2) from *The Puffin Book of Five-Minute Animal Stories* (Puffin) | W1, W2, T7, T8, T9, T14 |
| Modern stories with patterned language | **'What is the moon?'** (extracts 1 and 2) by Caroline Dunant from *Night, Night, Sleep Tight* (Red Fox) | W6, T12, T14 |
| Modern stories with predictable structures and patterned language | **'Down by the Cool of the Pool'** (extracts 1 and 2) from *Down by the Cool of the Pool* by Tony Mitton (Orchard Books) | W1, W6, T7, T8, T10 |
| Stories with patterned language | **'Farmyard Hullabaloo'** from *Cock-a-doodle-doo! Farmyard Hullabaloo* by Giles Andreae (Orchard Books) | W11, T6, T12, T15 |
| Poetry with patterned language | **'Rocket song'** by Barbara Ireson from *Over and Over Again* by Barbara Ireson and Christopher Rowe (Hamlyn) | W10, W11, T12 |
| | **'Early in the morning'** by Barbara Ireson from *Over and Over Again* by Barbara Ireson and Christopher Rowe (Hamlyn) | W6, W10, W11, T2, T12, T14 |
| | **'The Train Journey'** by Brenda Williams from *Around the Year* chosen by John Foster (Oxford University Press) | W2, W4, T11, T15 |
| Traditional poetry with predictable structures and patterned language | **'Five Busy Farmers'** from *One, Two, Skip a Few!* (Barefoot Books) | W1, W4, T3, T10 |
| Poetry with predictable structures and patterned language | **'One is a lion'** by Brenda Williams (previously unpublished) | W4, W6, T1, T10, T11 |
| | **'What is pink?'** from *Sing-Song: A Nursery Rhyme Book* by Christina Rossetti (Dover Publications) | W2, W11, T3, T10 |
| Nursery rhymes | **'Old Macdonald had a farm'** (Traditional) | W5, W11, T8, T10, T14 |
| Simple non-fiction texts | **'Signs that help us'** | W3, S4, T1, T11, T15 |
| | **'On the Farm'** from *On the Farm* by Henry Pluckrose (Franklin Watts) | W7, W10, T11 |
| | **'Take a Walk on a Rainbow'** from *Take a Walk on a Rainbow* by Miriam Moss (Macdonald Young Books) | W2, W6, T11 |

# The three little pigs

retold by Nikki Gamble

 *Extract 1*

## Background

The story of the three little pigs is a traditional English tale. The pattern of three occurs frequently in this type of story, being an economical way in which the moral point of the story can be made: two little pigs make quickly built, flimsy houses because they would rather play than work, but the third little pig's efforts show what can be achieved with perseverance and care. Links can be made to stories from other parts of the world. In American folklore there is a version in which Brer Rabbit outwits the wolf and there are similarities with the Grimms' *The Wolf and the Seven Little Kids*.

The text links with other extracts in this book: 'Goldilocks and the three bears' (page 22), 'The Three Billy Goats Gruff' (page 76) and 'Chicken Licken' (page 80).

## Shared reading and discussing the text

● Gather some straw, twigs and bricks to illustrate the materials the little pigs used for building their houses. Display a collection of different versions of the tale (see further reading suggestions below).
● Ask the children if they know the story of the three little pigs. Read the text, telling the children where you will start reading and pointing to the words as you read.
● After reading, ask whether the story so far is the same as the story they know. How is it the same? How is it different?
● The big bad wolf creeps up to the little pig's house. Ask if anyone can show how the wolf was creeping. Why was the wolf creeping? (So that he wouldn't be noticed; because he was up to no good; he wanted to take the little pigs by surprise.)
● What does the wolf ask the little pig? Why does the wolf want to get in to the house? Why does the little pig refuse to let the wolf in?
● Look at the opening words of the story. Do the children know any other stories that start with these words?

● Re-read the dialogue between the wolf and the little pig. Discuss how the characters would say the words. (For example, deep gruff voice for the wolf, high-pitched squeaky voice for the little pig.) Experiment with different voices and ask the children which they prefer.

## Activities

● Let the children work in pairs to improvise the scene between the wolf and the little pig.
● Ask the children to draw a picture of the wolf knocking at the little pig's house and caption it with *No! No!*. Show the children's work and re-read the caption together. Praise the children for recognising the word *No*. Add the word to the class word list or personal word banks.
● Write out the sentence *Take care and beware of the big bad wolf*. Ask the children to listen carefully as you read the sentence emphasising the *b* phoneme. Ask the children which words start with *b*. Suggest that the big bad wolf likes things that begin with *b*. Can they think of any other words that start with *b*?
● Introduce the concept of ordinal numbers using cut-out figures of the little pigs. Write the words *first, second* and *third* onto strips of card and attach them to the figures. Talk about the use of first, second and third in races or other competitions.

## Extension/further reading

Add to the list of the big bad wolf's things that begin with *b*. Create a display of objects and label them.

Develop the concept of ordinal numbers. Start with the figures of the three little pigs and then extend this to collections of toy cars, children in lines and so on.

Read other versions of the story, such as Nick Sharratt and Stephen Tucker's 'lift the flap' book (Macmillan Children's Books), Margaret Carter and Hilda Offen's *The Three Little Pigs and Other Stories* (Kingfisher), and by Ian Beck (OUP) and Paul Galdone (Houghton Mifflin).

**R W2:** knowledge of grapheme/phoneme correspondences through:
- hearing and identifying initial sounds in words
- reading letters that represent the sounds *a-z*

**R W6:** to read on sight the 45 high-frequency words to be taught by the end of YR from Appendix List 1

**R T3:** to re-read a text to provide context cues to help read unfamiliar words

*pattern of 3 common in traditional stories*

*traditional story language*

☐ = *high-frequency words*

*time connective; moves narrative on*

*direct speech*

*repetitive structure*

*ordinal numbers*

*effective movement verb*

*story language*

# The three little pigs   Extract 1

Once upon a time, three little pigs lived with their mother in a cottage at the edge of the woods.

One day their mother told them, "It is time for you to leave home and make your own way in the world."

So, off they went.

"Take care," Mother called as she waved goodbye, "and beware of the big bad wolf."

The first little pig built a house of straw. It didn't take her very long. Then she went out to play.

The second little pig built a house of sticks. It didn't take her very long either. Then she went out to play.

The third little pig worked very hard all day and built a house made with bricks. It was a good, strong house.

Later, the big bad wolf came out of the woods and crept up to the house made of straw.

He knocked at the door. RATATATTAT!

"Little pig, little pig, may I come in?"

"No! No!" By the hairs on my chinny chin chin I will not let you in!" the first little pig replied.

"Then I'll huff and I'll puff and I'll blow your house down!"

So the wolf huffed and puffed and blew the straw house down.

The little pig jumped up and ran to the house of sticks.

*alliterative*

*relates to the moral of the story*

*onomatopoeia; capital letters indicate loud noise*

**R T5:** to understand how story book language works, e.g. *'Once there was…'*

**R T8:** to locate and read significant parts of the text, e.g. names of key characters, chants

**R T12:** through guided and independent writing: to write labels or captions for pictures and drawings

# The three little pigs
retold by Nikki Gamble

## Background

In this second extract, hard work is rewarded and the big bad wolf gets his comeuppance. Traditionally, the wolf is the villain of the piece, although some modern retellings offer alternative moral viewpoints.

## Shared reading and discussing the text

● Ask the children to retell the first part of the story in pairs.

● Explain that the text you will be reading is the second half of the story. Ask the children where you should start reading. Check that they understand that you start in the top left-hand corner of the page and read along the line to the end before returning on the next line to the left-hand side of the page.

● Read aloud with expression to bring as much meaning to the text as possible. Encourage the children to join in with the chanting.

● Ask the children what sound is made when the wolf knocks at the door (*RATATATTAT!*). Ask if anyone can find the word. Remind them that it is written in capital letters to show that the knock is a very loud noise. Are there any other words in the story that are written in capital letters? Read the sentences aloud, emphasising the capitalised words.

● Mask some of the repeated words and phrases in paragraph two (for example *huff* and *puff*). Re-read the passage, stopping at the masked words. Ask the children to predict the words. Check their predictions each time by revealing the word. Draw attention to the construction of the word, especially the initial phonemes, and ask the children to listen to the difference between *huff* and *puff*.

● Talk about the ending of the story. Notice that the wolf cannot blow down the carefully built house of bricks, but he still gets in. Is it good that the wolf ends up in the cooking pot? Could the story end in another way? (Perhaps he goes away and never bothers the little pigs again, or he makes friends with them.) Ask the children to tell you about different endings from other versions they are familiar with.

## Activities

● Prepare large pictures of the wolf and the little pigs and add speech bubbles. In shared writing, ask the children what the wolf says when he knocks on the door of the little pig's house. Write these words in the speech bubble. Do the same for the little pig's reply.

● Ask the children to draw their favourite part of the story and encourage them to talk to you and each other about their pictures.

● In a circle, retell the whole story from memory. Each child should add a bit to the story before passing it on. A special storyteller's object (such as a toy pig) can be used to signal who is talking.

● Identify four or five main sentences from this retelling to construct a wall story. Write the sentences on cards and ask the children to illustrate them.

● Prepare a large sheet of paper with two circles in which to sort words. Label one of the circles *huff* and the other *puff*. Provide a set of cards with words that begin with *h* (such as *hat*, *hill*, *hot*, *hut*) and a set with words that begin with *p* (*pat*, *pill*, *pot*, *put*). Ask the children to sort the h words to put in the *huff* circle and the p words in the *puff* circle. An alternative version can be played with pictures of objects.

## Extension/further reading

Draw a set of characters from the story and attach a small piece of magnetic strip to the back of each one. Make the figures available with a magnetic board in the role-play area and encourage the children to use the characters to retell the story to each other.

Encourage browsing through books in the three little pigs display. Ask children to show their favourites and read them in story time.

More wolf and pig stories include *Suddenly!* by Colin McNaughton (Picture Lions), Peter and the Wolf by Ian Beck (Corgi), *Wicked Wolf Tales* by Laura Cecil and Emma Chichester Clark (Collins & Brown) and *The Three Little Wolves and the Big Bad Pig* by Eugene Trivizas and Helen Oxenbury (Mammoth).

**R W2:** knowledge of grapheme/ phoneme correspondences through hearing and identifying initial sounds in words

**R S2:** to use awareness of the grammar of a sentence to predict words during shared reading and when re-reading familiar stories

**R T1:** through shared reading: to track the text in the right order, page by page, left to right, top to bottom

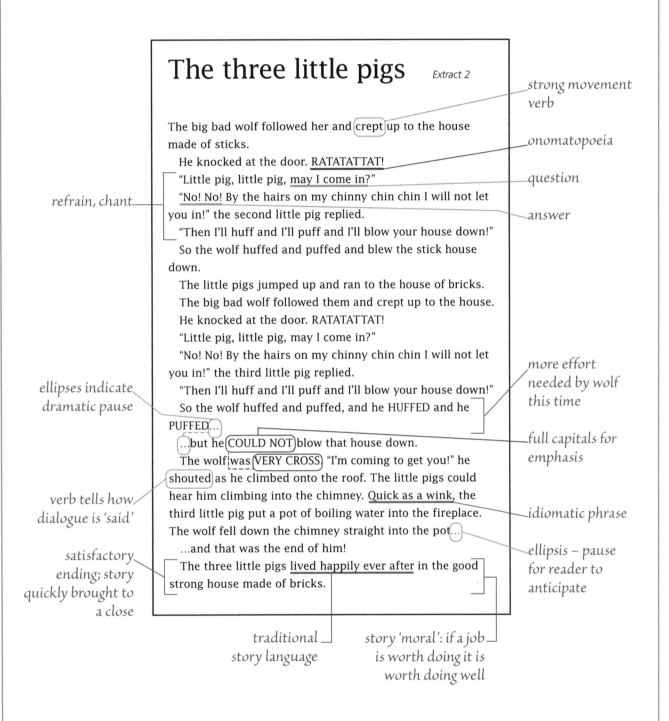

# The three little pigs

*Extract 2*

The big bad wolf followed her and crept up to the house made of sticks.

He knocked at the door. RATATATTAT!

"Little pig, little pig, may I come in?"

"No! No! By the hairs on my chinny chin chin I will not let you in!" the second little pig replied.

"Then I'll huff and I'll puff and I'll blow your house down!"

So the wolf huffed and puffed and blew the stick house down.

The little pigs jumped up and ran to the house of bricks.

The big bad wolf followed them and crept up to the house.

He knocked at the door. RATATATTAT!

"Little pig, little pig, may I come in?"

"No! No! By the hairs on my chinny chin chin I will not let you in!" the third little pig replied.

"Then I'll huff and I'll puff and I'll blow your house down!"

So the wolf huffed and puffed, and he HUFFED and he PUFFED...

...but he COULD NOT blow that house down.

The wolf was VERY CROSS "I'm coming to get you!" he shouted as he climbed onto the roof. The little pigs could hear him climbing into the chimney. Quick as a wink, the third little pig put a pot of boiling water into the fireplace. The wolf fell down the chimney straight into the pot...

...and that was the end of him!

The three little pigs lived happily ever after in the good strong house made of bricks.

strong movement verb

onomatopoeia

question

answer

refrain, chant

more effort needed by wolf this time

full capitals for emphasis

ellipses indicate dramatic pause

verb tells how dialogue is 'said'

idiomatic phrase

ellipsis – pause for reader to anticipate

satisfactory ending; story quickly brought to a close

traditional story language

story 'moral': if a job is worth doing it is worth doing well

**R T7:** to use knowledge of familiar texts to re-enact or retell to others, recounting the main points in correct sequence

**R T9:** to be aware of story structures, e.g. actions/reactions, consequences, and the ways that stories are built up and concluded

**R T10:** to re-read and recite stories with predictable and repeated patterns

# In the dark, dark town Traditional

### Background

This is a traditional story with a repetitive structure, which depends on the elements of suspense and surprise for its appeal. There are a number of illustrated and pop-up versions of the story, which make use of different endings (see suggestions for further reading below). The ending in this version has been left blank so that you and the children can complete it with your own ideas.

### Shared reading and discussing the text

● Prepare the text by drawing a picture to complete the blank at the end of the story (for example, a box of eggs, a ghost, a little mouse). Stick the illustration on the text, then mask it.

● Read the title. Draw the children's attention to the repeated use of the word *dark*. What kind of story do they think this will be?

● Read the story through with expression, emphasising the element of suspense. (A whisper will help build tension.) When you read the last line, whip off the masking device to emphasise the surprise.

● Discuss whether the ending was a surprise to the children. What did they expect to be in the cupboard? What would they like to put in the cupboard to end the story? Try out some of the suggestions by reading the last two lines each time.

● Relate the theme of surprises to personal experiences and encourage the children to tell you about good or bad surprises they have had.

● Consider ways of describing the dark (for example, *as dark as the night sky, as dark as a black hole, as dark as plain chocolate*).

● Re-read the text and ask the children to join in. Praise them for recognising the word *dark*.

### Activities

● In shared writing, produce a class version of the dark, dark story. Use a blank big book and write the *dark, dark* sentences at the bottom of the pages. Invite suggestions for the final surprise and select one. Ask the children to provide illustrations for the book.

● Prepare an enlarged version of the text for the role-play area. A collection of different illustrations can be made from pictures cut out of catalogues so that the children can select different endings for the story.

Generate new and invented words that rhyme with *dark* (such as *park* and *bark*). Ask the children to help you write a sentence that includes some of the rhyming words. Get them to notice the rime (*ark*) and recognise the different onsets (*d, p, b* and so on).

● Ask the children to point to the word *cupboard* in the text, then write it on the board. Ask the children if they can find the word *cup* inside *cupboard*. Highlight the word and write it out again. Sound each phoneme, *c-u-p*, as you write.

● The text is structured around different prepositions (*in, through*). Use a range of props to demonstrate the meaning of these and other prepositions. You could use a teddy bear and an old box. Put the teddy *in* the box, then *on* the box and *under* the box. In shared writing, write the sentence *The teddy is in the box.* Explain how you are writing the word *in*. Re-read the sentence together and praise the children for recognising *in*. Add this to the class word list or personal word banks.

### Extension/further reading

Develop work on prepositions and read Eric Hill's *Where's Spot?* (Puffin Books).

Read different versions of the story, such as: Ruth Brown's *A Dark, Dark Tale* (Red Fox) and Jessica Souhami's *In the Dark, Dark Wood* (Frances Lincoln). Other stories about the dark include Jill Tomlinson's *The Owl Who Was Afraid of the Dark* (Egmont).

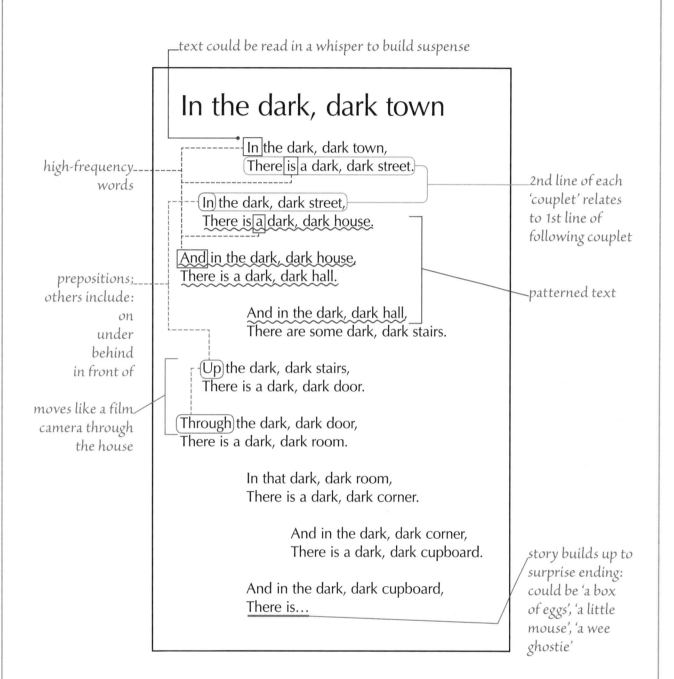

**R W4:** to link sound and spelling patterns by discriminating 'onsets' from 'rimes' in speech and spelling

**R W6:** to read on sight the 45 high-frequency words to be taught by the end of YR from Appendix List 1

*text could be read in a whisper to build suspense*

# In the dark, dark town

In the dark, dark town,
There is a dark, dark street.

In the dark, dark street,
There is a dark, dark house.

And in the dark, dark house,
There is a dark, dark hall.

And in the dark, dark hall,
There are some dark, dark stairs.

Up the dark, dark stairs,
There is a dark, dark door.

Through the dark, dark door,
There is a dark, dark room.

In that dark, dark room,
There is a dark, dark corner.

And in the dark, dark corner,
There is a dark, dark cupboard.

And in the dark, dark cupboard,
There is…

*high-frequency words*

*prepositions; others include:*
*on*
*under*
*behind*
*in front of*

*moves like a film camera through the house*

*2nd line of each 'couplet' relates to 1st line of following couplet*

*patterned text*

*story builds up to surprise ending: could be 'a box of eggs', 'a little mouse', 'a wee ghostie'*

**R T6:** to re-read frequently a variety of familiar texts, e.g. big books, story books, poems

**R T9:** to be aware of story structures e.g. actions/reactions, consequences, and the ways that stories are built-up and concluded

**R T10:** to re-read and recite stories and rhymes with predictable and repeated patterns and experiment with similar rhyming patterns

# Grumble-Rumble!

by Siobhan Dodds

*Extracts 1 and 2*

## Background

These extracts are taken from the beginning and end of a picture book in which Little Roo is too busy to have breakfast and she becomes convinced that a monster is following her. She visits a sequence of friends, but all are too busy eating their breakfast to take much account of Little Roo's concerns. This patterned story has a repeating structure based on a journey, which can be extended during shared writing. The story also provides an opportunity for discussing healthy eating issues.

The story's food theme can be used to link with the following texts in this term: 'Sounds Good' (page 24), 'Party invitation' (page 30), 'Menu' (page 32), 'Cooking rules' (page 34) and 'Chocolate apples' (page 36).

## Shared reading and discussing the text

● Relate the theme of the story to personal experience by talking to the children about their favourite breakfast foods. Explain that you are going to read a story about a little kangaroo who will not eat her breakfast.

● Check the children's understanding of how books work and how sentences should be read. Ask them to show you where you should start reading and what happens when you reach the end of a line.

● Read the extracts aloud. Check that the children understand that the grumble-rumble was Little Roo's stomach rumbling. Why was it rumbling? (Because she hadn't eaten her breakfast.) Briefly discuss the 'moral' of the story. (Eat your breakfast before you go out to play – you can't play on an empty stomach.)

● Ask the children if they were surprised that the crocodile was eating grapes for breakfast. What would they expect a crocodile to eat?

● Ask a volunteer to point to one instance of the words GRUMBLE-RUMBLE! Why are these words printed differently to the other words? How should these words be read? Practise reading the words in different voices (loudly, in a whisper, slowly, quickly and so on) and decide which sounds most appropriate to the story.

● To develop the children's vocabulary and understanding of animals, re-read the sentence *'A monster!' cried Little Roo, and bounced off to tell her friend Crocodile.* Consider why Little Roo *bounces* off. (Because she is a kangaroo.) Think about the way other animals in the story would move. What about Crocodile? What about Snake? Extend the list by telling the children that Roo then goes to visit Elephant, Lion and Monkey and considering other animals with which the children are familiar. You could also let the children's imaginations run on what the various animal characters might eat.

## Activities

● In shared writing, construct a sequence of episodes to extend the story. What happens when Little Roo visits Snake? Who might she visit next? A new paragraph can be added to the story each day. Use the new episodes to make an illustrated big book and make it available in the role-play or reading area.

● Prepare pictures of Little Roo, her mother and Crocodile and add speech bubbles in shared writing, using the dialogue given in the text. For example, Little Roo says to Crocodile, *There's a monster following me.* Write her sentence inside the speech bubble. Do the same for Mummy Roo.

● In pairs, ask the children to tell each other the story. Record the retellings and play them back to the children afterwards.

● Ask the children to draw their favourite breakfast and encourage them to caption their drawings.

## Extension/further reading

Create a display on healthy eating with pictures of nutritious breakfast food, packets and labels.

Read the full text of *Grumble-Rumble!* and other books by Siobhan Dodds, such as *Squeak! Squeak!* (Hodder Children's Books) and *Grandad Pot* (Walker Books). A book with a similar theme is Ronda and David Armitage's *The Lighthouse Keeper's Breakfast* (Scholastic).

# Grumble-Rumble!

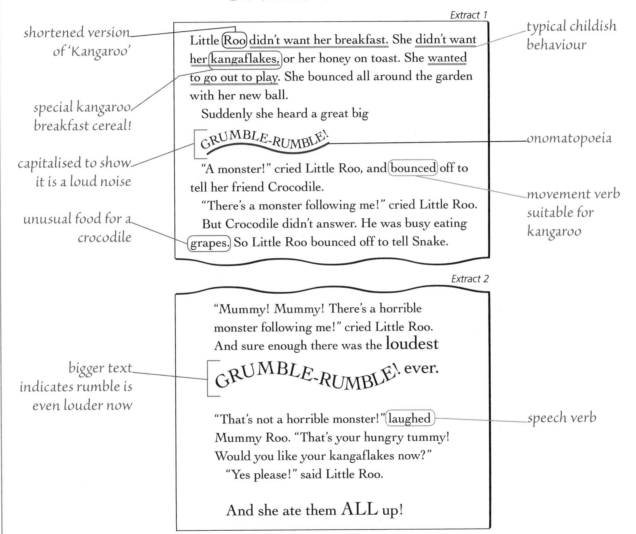

*Extract 1*

shortened version of 'Kangaroo'

special kangaroo breakfast cereal!

capitalised to show it is a loud noise

unusual food for a crocodile

typical childish behaviour

onomatopoeia

movement verb suitable for kangaroo

Little Roo didn't want her breakfast. She didn't want her kangaflakes, or her honey on toast. She wanted to go out to play. She bounced all around the garden with her new ball.

Suddenly she heard a great big

GRUMBLE-RUMBLE!

"A monster!" cried Little Roo, and bounced off to tell her friend Crocodile.

"There's a monster following me!" cried Little Roo. But Crocodile didn't answer. He was busy eating grapes. So Little Roo bounced off to tell Snake.

*Extract 2*

bigger text indicates rumble is even louder now

speech verb

"Mummy! Mummy! There's a horrible monster following me!" cried Little Roo. And sure enough there was the loudest

GRUMBLE-RUMBLE! ever.

"That's not a horrible monster!" laughed Mummy Roo. "That's your hungry tummy! Would you like your kangaflakes now?"

"Yes please!" said Little Roo.

And she ate them ALL up!

# I Like Me!

## by Babs Bell Hajdusiewicz

### Background

'I Like Me!' conveys a positive message about liking oneself, a message intended to promote a good self-image and esteem.

The structure is a list poem, with most of the lines starting with the words *I like*. The predictable pattern provides a supportive structure for generating shared and guided writing. Many of the words are included in the NLS high-frequency word list (*I, like, look, play, was, me*). The rhyme scheme (rhyming couplets) makes the poem an ideal starting point for the oral prediction and generation of rhyme.

This poem can link with other texts in this term: 'Painting' (page 20), 'My Bed' (page 28) and 'My body' (page 40).

### Shared reading and discussing the text

● Share with the children one thing that you like about yourself. Then ask them to think of one thing they like about themselves. Encourage them to offer their thoughts.

● Show the text to the children and read it with expression, emphasising the celebratory tone of the poem (each line ending with an exclamation mark). Ask the children to follow the words as you read, to match the spoken words with the written text.

● Read the poem a second time and encourage the children to join in. Pause at the rhyming words to encourage prediction.

● Draw attention to the capitalised *ME!* at the end, and to the explanation mark. This tells us to read these words very loudly. Demonstrate how to read the last three lines. Then read the poem together showing how loudly *ME!* can be read!

### Activities

● On a large sheet of paper, write the title, the first line and the first two words of the second line of the poem, sounding out phonemes as you write. Use this frame to begin a class poem, using the children's suggestions on how to finish each *I like...* (It isn't necessary for the poem to rhyme.) Return to the text and ask the children if they can recognise the words *I like*. Add these words to the class word list or personal word banks.

● Re-read the third and fourth lines. Repeat the rhyming words *today/play*. Ask the children for other words that sound like *play*. Generate more rhymes orally (include new and invented words as appropriate).

● Play a 'Pass the rhyme' game. Sit in a circle and clap a slow beat. Invite the children to join in. Start the rhyming string: *today/play/may...* The child on the left continues the rhyme and then the child on their left and so on around the circle. Tell the children that you have created a rhyming string and ask whether anyone knows what the term *rhyme* means. The activity can be repeated for other rhymes in the poem.

● Ask the children to draw one or two self-portraits showing things that they like about themselves. Encourage them to write captions. (For example, *I'm kind to my rabbit, I help my mum, I'm good at swimming.*) Invite them to talk about their pictures during circle time or with an adult.

### Extension/further reading

Each child could make an illustrated zigzag book entitled 'All About Me' to share with parents and carers.

Regularly read further rhymes and simple rhyming poetry to extend the children's rhyming repertoire. Look for collections of poetry and verse that the children can easily relate to, such as *Twinkle Twinkle Chocolate Bar* and *Rhyme Time: Around the day*, both compiled by John Foster (OUP).

**R W1:** to understand and be able to rhyme through:
● recognising, exploring and working with rhyming patterns
● extending these patterns by analogy, generating new and invented words in speech and spelling

**R W6:** to read on sight the 45 high-frequency words to be taught by the end of YR from Appendix List 1

*the voice/speaker of the poem is a child*

*patterned structure*

☐ *= high-frequency words*

*splitting last line into 3 slows the pace and gives emphasis to final thought*

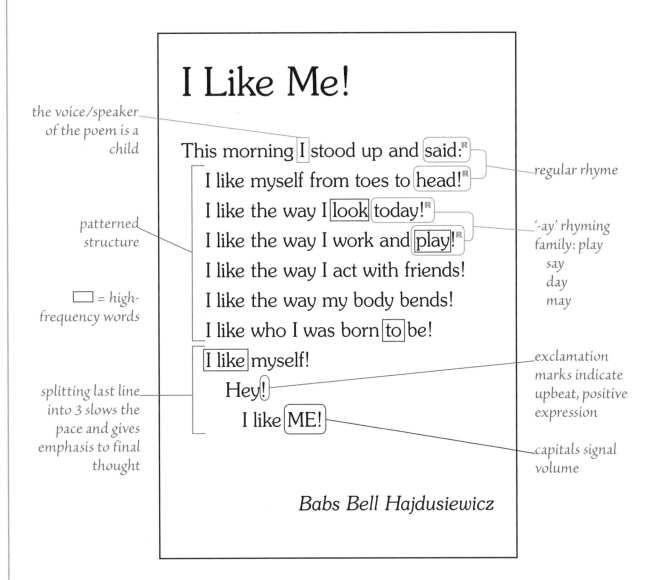

# I Like Me!

This morning I stood up and said:
  I like myself from toes to head!
  I like the way I look today!
  I like the way I work and play!
  I like the way I act with friends!
  I like the way my body bends!
  I like who I was born to be!
  I like myself!
    Hey!
    I like ME!

*Babs Bell Hajdusiewicz*

*regular rhyme*

*'-ay' rhyming family: play*
          *say*
          *day*
          *may*

*exclamation marks indicate upbeat, positive expression*

*capitals signal volume*

**R T10:** to re-read and recite stories and rhymes with predictable and repeated patterns and experiment with similar rhyming patterns

**R T12:** through guided and independent writing: to write labels or captions for pictures and drawings

# Painting

by Linda Hammond

## Background

This is an action rhyme with patterned features (sentence structure and rhyme). Humour is employed throughout and particularly in the final line where it becomes evident that so much paint has got onto the child there is none left for the intended purpose. The text provides an opportunity to introduce topic words (colour and parts of the body), and the actions and repeated words encourage the development of sight vocabulary. The rhythm is simple, consisting mainly of fairly short lines of monosyllabic words. This makes it an ideal verse for introducing rhythm clapping.

See 'I Like Me!' (page 18) for linking suggestions.

## Shared reading and discussing the text

● Build on the children's prior experience of painting. Talk with them about whether they enjoy painting. Do they make a mess when they paint? Do they get any on themselves? Where? Are they good about cleaning up afterwards?

● Prepare a copy of the poem, masking the actions written in italic. Read through the poem and teach the children the accompanying actions. Emphasise the humour in the last line. Read the poem a second time together, encouraging the children to join in and pausing to allow time to include the actions.

● Re-read the rhyme, this time asking the children to clap as you read it. The class could be divided in two, with one half clapping the first verse and the other half clapping the second. Clap the words *really* and *yellow* to show the contrast with the monosyllabic words. Some children may require more support in being able to detect rhythm. You can do this by slowing the pace and exaggerating the beats in the lines.

● Re-read the poem again, with the actions uncovered. Make sure the children can see the distinction in the way these are presented compared with the text of the poem. Draw attention to the hand actions *Wipe*, *Stroke*, *Touch*, *Point*. Ask the children what other actions you can perform with your hands. (Lift, hold, clap, wave, pat, write and so on.)

## Activities

● Working with a group of children, display an enlarged copy of the text with a large outline of a child. Explain that the poor child has lost all of his or her lovely colour and they are going to help put it back. Recite the poem together to remind the children of the words. Provide paint and ask the group to paint the figure according to the poem.

● Prepare pieces of coloured card (red, green, blue, black and yellow). Play a game of 'Hunt the colour'. Explain to the children that you are going to recite the rhyme together and when they hear/say a colour word they should raise their hand. Stop as each colour word is identified and, with the children's help, write the word on an appropriately coloured piece of card. Attach the labels to the painting of the figure.

● Create a hands display. Ask the children to draw around their hands and then cut out the shape. Make a display with the different hand shapes. Caption the display with *My hands. I can wipe, stroke, touch, point* plus words supplied by the children.

● Play a 'Simple Simon' action game using the hand actions used in the display. For example, *Simple Simon says point in the air*; *Simple Simon Says touch your nose*.

## Extension/further reading

Write colour words on pieces of white card. Ask the children to work in pairs to attach the cards to objects in the classroom of those colours.

Read a range of action rhymes, such as Elizabeth Matterson's compilation *This Little Puffin...* (Puffin Books), Zita Newcome's *Five Little Ducks* (Walker Books) and John Foster's *First Verses: Action Rhymes* (OUP).

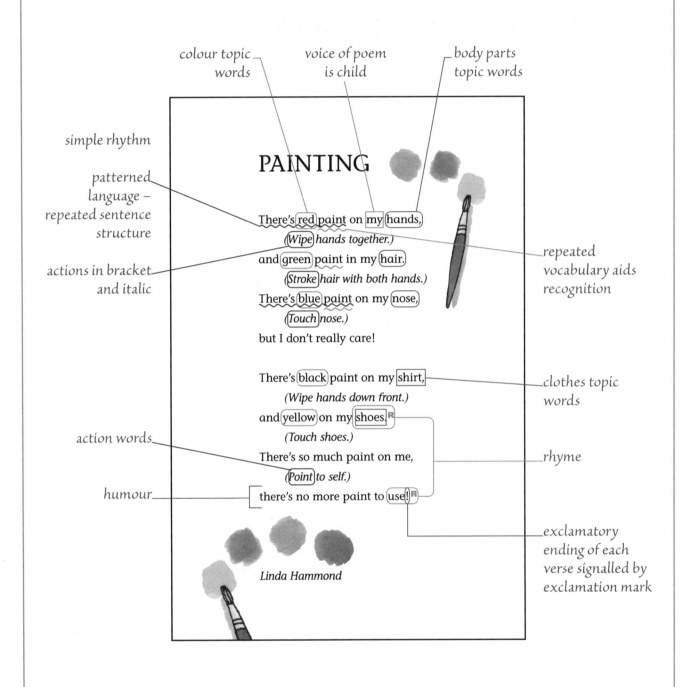

R W11: to make collections of personal interest or significant words and words linked to particular topics

colour topic words

voice of poem is child

body parts topic words

simple rhythm

patterned language – repeated sentence structure

actions in bracket and italic

## PAINTING

There's red paint on my hands,
(Wipe hands together.)
and green paint in my hair.
(Stroke hair with both hands.)
There's blue paint on my nose,
(Touch nose.)
but I don't really care!

There's black paint on my shirt,
(Wipe hands down front.)
and yellow on my shoes,
(Touch shoes.)
There's so much paint on me,
(Point to self.)
there's no more paint to use!

Linda Hammond

repeated vocabulary aids recognition

clothes topic words

action words

rhyme

humour

exclamatory ending of each verse signalled by exclamation mark

R T8: to locate and read significant parts of the text, e.g. italicised words

R T10: to re-read and recite rhymes with predictable and repeated patterns

# Goldilocks and the three bears
by Carolyn Sherwin Bailey

## Background

This is a popular counting rhyme version of the well-known traditional story. As well as numbers one to three, it includes words that can be used to order size (*huge, small* and *tiny*). The repeated chorus and patterned verses provide a supportive framework for the children to join in and extend their recognition of high-frequency words. The children may recognise the rhyme from nursery or home.

An audio version is available (see Further reading below) if the tune is not familiar.

## Shared reading and discussing the text

● Ask whether anyone knows the story of Goldilocks and the three bears. Either tell the story to the children or construct a retelling with them.

● Read the rhymed version and talk about the story. Do the children like it? Which parts do they like best? Do they think Goldilocks behaved badly or not in this version? (We are only told that she *saw* the bears' things.) Do they think she was frightened when the bears growled at her?

● Point out the question and answer structure of the poem, which uses repetitions of the chorus from the beginning. Draw attention to the final line and ask the children how the capitalised words should be read. Notice the exclamation marks that add emphasis too. Practise reading this line in different ways and decide which sounds best.

● Re-read the text, pausing to allow the children to predict significant and repeated words.

## Activities

● Create a wall story based on the rhyme. In three groups, ask the children to draw a picture for each of the episodes (bowls, chairs, beds) and help them to caption them with lines from the poem (*A bowl that was huge...*).

● Use a similar question and answer structure to write some sentences about other well-known folk tales and nursery rhymes. For example, *When Little Red Riding Hood went to her grandma's cottage, what did she see? When the Billy Goats Gruff stepped onto the bridge, what did they see? When Humpty Dumpty sat on his wall, what did he see?*). Emphasise the word *see*, drawing attention to its construction as you write.

● Re-read the text and point out that the bears and their belongings were different sizes. Draw a huge bear, a small bear and a tiny bear and label them with the words *huge, small* and *tiny*. Explain that the words describe different sizes. Ask the children to draw the three bears in their house with their different-sized bowls, chairs and beds. Ask them to label their pictures with the key words.

● To develop recognition of the word *went* from the text, ask the children, *Where did Goldilocks go?* Write the answer, speaking the words as you write: *Goldilocks went to the three bears' house.*

● Re-read one of the verses. Ask the children to listen and tell you which words rhyme. (*Small* and *all*.) Play a 'Pass the rhyme' game (see page 18) with the *all* rhyming family.

● Re-enact the story in a 'walk-through talk-through'. (The children enact the story as you tell it.) Incorporate words from the rhymed version into the telling and encourage the children to use suitable actions to show Goldilocks looking around and the relative sizes of the beds and chairs, for example.

● In a hot-seating activity, take on the role of Goldilocks and encourage the children to ask you questions about what you did and why. Ask the children if Goldilocks could make friends with the three bears. In pairs (one as Goldilocks and one as tiny bear), role-play Goldilocks and tiny bear meeting and making friends.

## Extension/further reading

Read a prose version of 'Goldilocks and the Three Bears', such as by Tony Mitton and Liz Million (Walker Books), Ian Beck (OUP), Susan Price and Rosalind Beardshaw (CUP Big Book).

**R W1:** to understand and be able to rhyme through: recognising, exploring and working with rhyming patterns

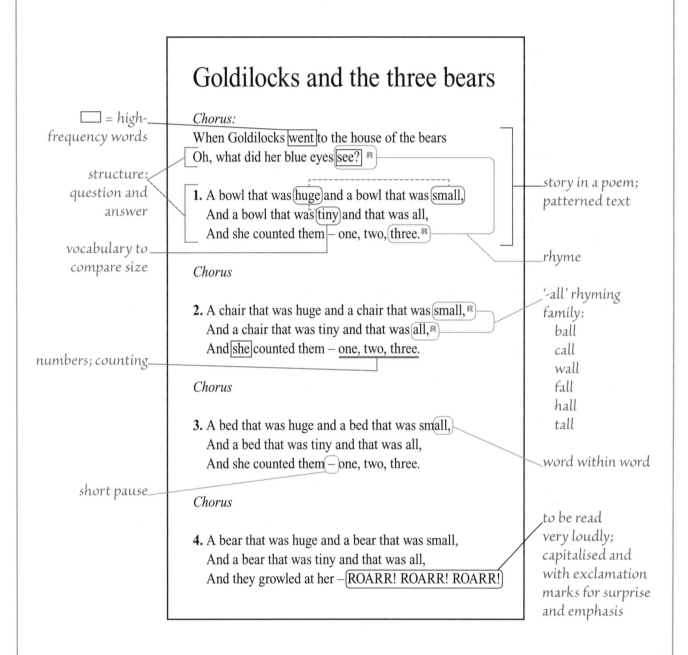

# Goldilocks and the three bears

☐ = high-frequency words

structure: question and answer

vocabulary to compare size

numbers; counting

short pause

*Chorus:*

When Goldilocks went to the house of the bears
Oh, what did her blue eyes see? ᴿ

1. A bowl that was huge and a bowl that was small,
   And a bowl that was tiny and that was all,
   And she counted them – one, two, three. ᴿ

*Chorus*

2. A chair that was huge and a chair that was small, ᴿ
   And a chair that was tiny and that was all, ᴿ
   And she counted them – one, two, three.

*Chorus*

3. A bed that was huge and a bed that was small,
   And a bed that was tiny and that was all,
   And she counted them – one, two, three.

*Chorus*

4. A bear that was huge and a bear that was small,
   And a bear that was tiny and that was all,
   And they growled at her – ROARR! ROARR! ROARR!

story in a poem; patterned text

rhyme

'-all' rhyming family:
   ball
   call
   wall
   fall
   hall
   tall

word within word

to be read very loudly; capitalised and with exclamation marks for surprise and emphasis

**R W6:** to read on sight the 45 high-frequency words to be taught by the end of YR from Appendix List 1

**R T10:** to re-read and recite stories and rhymes with predictable and repeated patterns and experiment with similar rhyming patterns

# Sounds Good

by Judith Nicholls

### Background

This simple poem uses a list structure and easy-to-follow rhythm. It employs a lot of alliteration and onomatopoeia to bring the cooking and eating images to life. Children will appreciate the mouth-watering effect of the build up of sounds. No wonder the poet says *I'm hungry* with such emphasis at the end of the poem!

### Shared reading and discussing the text

● Read the poem, encouraging the children to catch the rhythm and notice the rhyme. Emphasise how the words mimic the sound of cooking. Ask the children if they enjoyed the poem and what they particularly liked about it.

● Identify the various sounds different foods make in the poem (*sizzle, crack, hiss* and so on). Experiment with different ways of saying the words, emphasising onomatopoeic qualities.

● Point out the three dots (ellipsis) used to indicate a dramatic pause before the last line. Model how to read the last stanza and closing line, emphasising the pause.

● Ask the children to find the words written in capital letters. Choose one child to underline the words and ask the rest of the class to check if the correct words have been underlined. Ask the children why they think these words have been written in capital letters. (For example, because they are the start of sentences.)

● To help the children to hear and identify initial sounds in words, pick out alliterative words from the text, such as *bacon boils, baked beans bubble*. Ask the children if they can hear which sound the words begin with. Make up a new sentence containing mainly words beginning with *b*, for example *Bobby blew bubbles in the bath. Belinda bought a blue balloon*. Practise saying it with the children, pointing out the *b* each time.

### Activities

● Gather a collection of percussion instruments and materials for creating sound effects (such as bubble wrap, a glass of water with a straw, tin foil). Ask the children to choose something that will make a bubbling sound and to demonstrate how to make the sound. Do the same for other sound words from the poem. Re-read the poem, using the sound words to cue the different instruments.

● In small groups, ask the children to cut pictures of food out of magazines and stick them onto card to make a collage. Help them to add sound words to the collage. These can be written independently or scribed on strips of paper and then attached.

● In shared writing, write another verse for the poem. What foods do the children enjoy? What other foods make noise? Use real and invented words to describe the sounds, such as *corn flakes crunching, porridge glooping*. Encourage alliteration where possible.

● Give three children large cards with *b, p* and *g* on them. Ask the children to stand in different parts of the room. Give the rest of the class objects beginning with the phonemes, for example ball, box, banana, pen, plum, pencil, glove, glue (use hard *g* only). Ask the children to take their object and stand with the child holding the letter that their object begins with. Ask each child in turn to name their object and ask the class to confirm that the child is in the correct place. The game can be adapted for words ending with the same phonemes (*mug, bag, peg, cup, cap* and so on).

### Extension/further reading

In dance, develop movements to accompany the contrasting sound words *bubble, squelch, crack* and *hiss*. Take each word in turn and experiment with different speeds, directions and levels. Accompany a re-reading of the poem with the movements.

Play a 'bean' game. Different beans have different actions: runner bean runs clockwise around the room; jumping bean jumps on the spot; baked bean lies down as if sunbathing; jelly bean shivers like jelly. Call out bean names for the children to perform the actions.

Read John Foster's collection *Egg Poems* and Jill Bennett's *Tasty Poems* (both OUP).

**R W2:** knowledge of grapheme/phoneme correspondences through:
● hearing and identifying initial sounds in words
● reading letters that represent the sounds

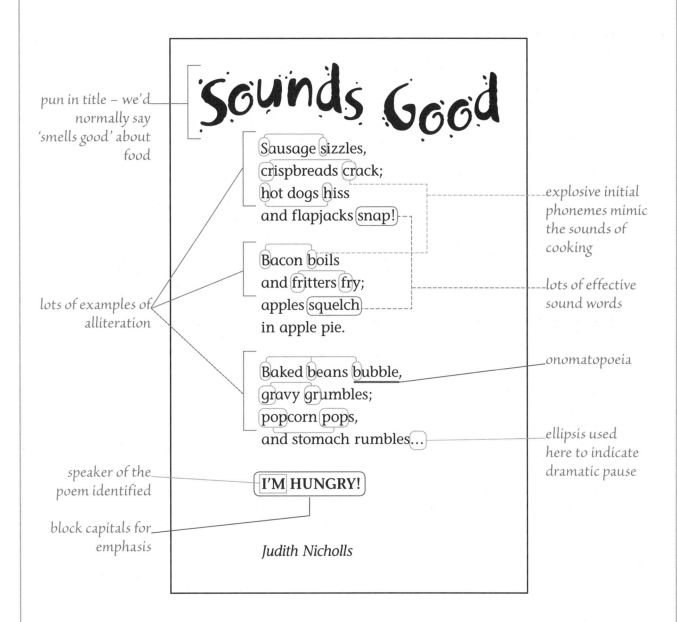

pun in title – we'd normally say 'smells good' about food

# Sounds Good

Sausage sizzles,
crispbreads crack;
hot dogs hiss
and flapjacks snap!

explosive initial phonemes mimic the sounds of cooking

Bacon boils
and fritters fry;
apples squelch
in apple pie.

lots of effective sound words

lots of examples of alliteration

Baked beans bubble,
gravy grumbles;
popcorn pops,
and stomach rumbles…

onomatopoeia

ellipsis used here to indicate dramatic pause

speaker of the poem identified

**I'M HUNGRY!**

block capitals for emphasis

*Judith Nicholls*

**R W4:** to link sound and spelling patterns by:
● discriminating 'onsets' from 'rhymes'
● identifying alliteration in known and new and invented words

**R T14:** to use experience of stories, poems and simple recounts as a basis for independent writing, e.g. retelling, substitution, extension, and through shared composition with adults

# Bedtime

by Eleanor Farjeon

## Background

This classic poem by Eleanor Farjeon (1881–1965) describes an experience that will be as familiar to children today as it was to its original audience. It is written in the voice of a child in a direct appeal to an adult. The child asks a series of questions in an attempt to stay up beyond his or her bedtime. Children can be invited to reflect on their own experiences of similar situations. More broadly, they can be encouraged to listen to and record the words that people say in different situations (for example, when getting ready for school).

The poem uses a repetitive structure and simple rhythm that encourages children to join in and predict when reading.

## Shared reading and discussing the text

● Talk about bedtime routines. Are there particular things that the children like to do before bedtime, such as listen to a story? Reinforce the importance of bedtime routines, such as cleaning teeth.

● Relate the poem to the children's experiences. Have they ever tried to persuade an adult to let them stay up later (or buy them a toy, ice cream and so on)? What did they say? What did the adult say? Write some of these expressions in large speech bubbles. These can be displayed later with the children's artwork.

● Read the poem with expression to emphasise the pleading tone.

● Talk with the children about their favourite parts of the poem. Ask which of the reasons mentioned would be most likely to persuade an adult to let the child stay up a bit later.

● Draw attention to the italicised words. Re-read the lines containing these words. Ask the children if they notice anything about the way the lines sounded when they were read aloud. In pairs, let the children practise reciting the lines with appropriate expression.

## Activities

● Use the text as a model for writing a class poem. Ask the children to tell you what things they say to try to persuade an adult to let them stay up later than their usual bedtime. Write their questions, and exclamations, on the board, drawing attention to the question mark and exclamation mark at the end of each question. Assemble the questions to create the poem – the poem need not rhyme like the original.

● Ask the children to draw a picture showing the activities mentioned in the poem. Alternatively, ask them to draw their own favourite activities. Are any the same as the ones in the poem?

● Re-read the four lines *Can't I just finish the story…* Ask the children to identify the rhyming words (*book/look*). Generate more rhymes in the same family, real and invented (for example, *took*, *cook*, *hook*). Repeat the activity with other rhyming pairs in the poem. More experienced readers can consider whether words need to be spelled the same in order to sound the same.

## Extension/further reading

Practise counting backwards from five (*five minutes, four minutes…*). Extend this to countdown from 10 or 20 as appropriate.

How long is a minute? Show the children an analogue clock with a second hand. Explain that the hand moves through a complete circle in one minute. Ask the children if they think they can be quiet for one whole minute. When the second hand reaches 12, time a minute's silence. Did it seem like a long or short time?

Other poems by Eleanor Farjeon such as 'Cats' (see page 60) and 'Morning Has Broken' are in the collection *Morning Has Broken* (Eedermans). *The Little Bookroom* (OUP) is a collection of her children's stories. Robert Louis Stevenson's 'Bed in Summer' in *A Child's Garden of Verses* provides an interesting contrast to 'Bedtime'. Michael Rosen's poetry often includes 'conversations' in different situations; see, for example, *Wouldn't You Like to Know* and *Mind Your Own Business* (both Scholastic).

**R W1:** to understand and be able to rhyme through:
● exploring and working with rhyming patterns
● extending these patterns by analogy, generating new and invented words in speech and spelling

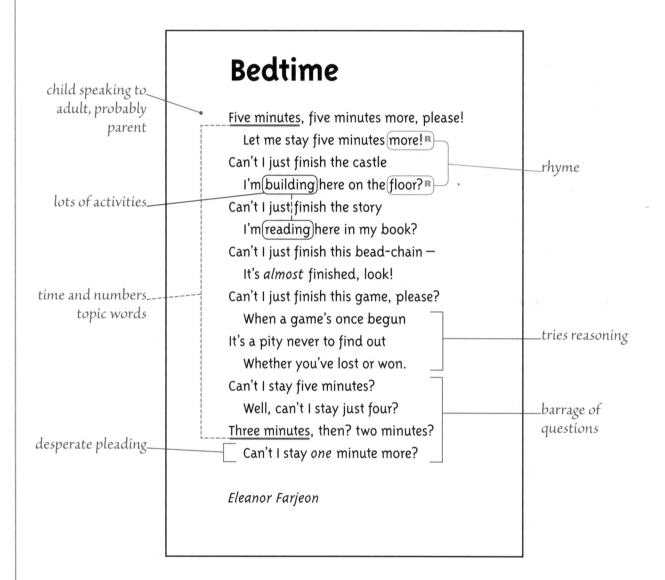

child speaking to adult, probably parent

lots of activities

time and numbers topic words

desperate pleading

# Bedtime

Five minutes, five minutes more, please!
    Let me stay five minutes more!
Can't I just finish the castle
    I'm building here on the floor?
Can't I just finish the story
    I'm reading here in my book?
Can't I just finish this bead-chain —
    It's *almost* finished, look!
Can't I just finish this game, please?
    When a game's once begun
It's a pity never to find out
    Whether you've lost or won.
Can't I stay five minutes?
    Well, can't I stay just four?
Three minutes, then? two minutes?
    Can't I stay *one* minute more?

*Eleanor Farjeon*

rhyme

tries reasoning

barrage of questions

**R T12:** through guided and independent writing: to write their own names

**R W8:** to read and write own name and explore other words related to the spelling of own name

**R S4:** to use a capital letter for the start of own name

# My Bed

by Tony Mitton

## Background

'My Bed' is written with a child's eye view of the world; an imaginative world in which a bed can be an island, a boat, a car or a rocket.

The regular ABCB rhyme scheme can be exploited to encourage the children to predict rhyming words. The poem can also introduce children to figurative language, as a simile is used in each verse to express the idea that a bed can be whatever the child chooses.

Most of the images are very active (boats, racing car, rocket), but the final verse contrasts this by creating an image of diving deep below the sea as the child slows down and enters the depths of sleep.

## Shared reading and discussing the text

● Share a story from your own childhood about the imaginative games you used to play. Then draw on the children's similar experiences of imaginative play, encouraging them to talk about their imaginary worlds.

● Read 'My Bed'. Have any of the children ever imagined that their bed was something else? An island surrounded by shark-infested seas? A secret den? A space capsule?

● Read the poem a second time, pausing to encourage the children to predict the rhyming words. Notice that these are all nouns.

● Talk about some of the action words (verbs) and clarify definitions if necessary: ask the children if they can float along in the swimming pool; explain roaring as the loud, deep sound made by the car engine as it speeds away and diving as exploring underwater. Some children might also know that you can dive into water from a diving board. Compose some new sentences containing these words, for example Jack can float in the swimming pool. The lion roared fiercely. Emphasise the action words.

● The word bed is repeated frequently. Ask one of the children to find the word. Then ask another child to look for another instance of bed in a different place in the poem.

## Activities

● Ask the children to draw or paint one of the images from the poem using a choice of materials and media. In circle time, encourage the children to talk about their artwork or talk with the children on a one-to-one basis about their paintings.

● Help the children to compose another verse of the poem with their own imaginative ideas or memories of what their bed could be. Advise them to use the poem as a model and to think about where their bed might take them and what they might do. Remind them to use the line starters My bed, And now, or give them a writing frame.

● Re-read the alliterative line diving down deep, emphasising the initial phoneme d. Ask the children to listen carefully to the beginning of each word. Then give them a collection of objects, some of which begin with d. Ask the children to hold up their objects if they begin with the same letter as the words diving down deep. Display the collection of objects beginning with d and ask the children to help you label them.

● Start with the word bed and substitute initial phonemes in order to discover new words. Ask the children to generate a list of as many words they can think of that rhyme with bed.

## Extension/further reading

Watch and talk about the scene in Bedknobs and Broomsticks (Disney Home Video) where the brass bed magically transports the children under the sea.

The repertoire of poetry can be extended by reading more poems that present a child's imaginative view of the world, such as Robert Louis Stevenson's A Child's Garden of Verses (especially 'The Land of Counterpane' in which a bed is transformed into a landscape for play), My Dream Bed by Lauren Child (Hodder Children's Books) and Night Lights: 24 Poems to Sleep On by Denys Cazet (Orchard).

**R W1:** to understand and be able to rhyme through:
● recognising, exploring and working with rhyming patterns
● extending these patterns by analogy, generating new and invented words in speech and spelling

**R W4:** to link sound and spelling patterns by: using knowledge of rhyme to identify families of rhyming CVC words

written from child's point of view

simple similes in each verse create easily identifiable images

action vocabulary

noise

contrasts directions of movement

alliteration

ABCB rhyme scheme

forms of transport

choice of similes suit child's imagination being presented

pace slows

satisfying conclusion

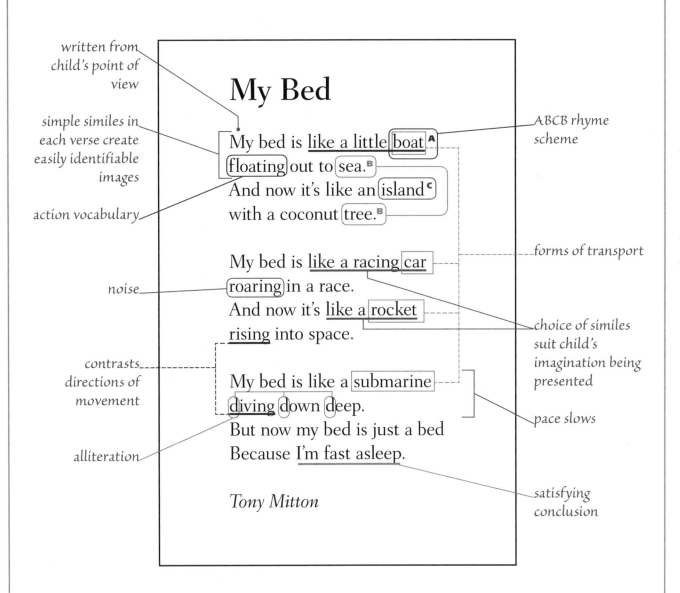

# My Bed

My bed is like a little boat <sup>A</sup>
floating out to sea.<sup>B</sup>
And now it's like an island <sup>C</sup>
with a coconut tree.<sup>B</sup>

My bed is like a racing car
roaring in a race.
And now it's like a rocket
rising into space.

My bed is like a submarine
diving down deep.
But now my bed is just a bed
Because I'm fast asleep.

*Tony Mitton*

**R S2:** to use awareness of the grammar of a sentence to predict words during shared reading and when re-reading familiar texts

**R T3:** to re-read a text to provide context cues to help read unfamiliar words

**R T14:** to use experience of stories, poems and simple recounts as a basis for independent writing, e.g. retelling, substitution, extension, and through shared composition with adults

# Party invitation

## Background

Receiving party invitations is a common occurrence in many children's experience. Invitations can be used to introduce children to genuine purposes for writing. Suggested activities provide opportunities for sending and receiving invitations, thus reinforcing that this type of communication has a tangible outcome. Most invitations follow a similar layout and shorthand style, containing the information of who, what, where and when.

## Shared reading and discussing the text

● Ask the children to bring in any party invitations they have received and kept, and create a display of them.
● Ask the children to talk about any invitations they have received or sent. *Why do we send invitations? What kinds of decoration do they have?* (For example, pictures of birthday cakes, footballs, film characters.) Illustrate the discussion with examples from the display.
● Read the invitation together. Show that some of the words are printed and some are handwritten and ask the children why. Note the clear layout and that only essential information is given. Explain that the reader can see quickly what he needs to know.
● Why is it important to put the date and the time of the party? What about the name of the venue and its address? (What would happen if the invitation just said *Pizza Place*? How would you know which one to go to?) Explain that RSVP means 'please reply'. Consider why you should reply to an invitation. (It is polite, it is important for the person holding the party to know how many people to expect.)
● Show a blank party invitation. Draw attention to the words *at* and *on*. Ask the children how many sounds they can hear in *at*. Say the word slowly, emphasising the two phonemes. Then write the word, pronouncing the phonemes as you write. Repeat this for *on*. Add the words to the class word list or personal word banks.
● Ask the children to help you complete the details on the blank invitation.

## Activities

● In shared writing, write a reply to the invitation, using a large, blank card. Explain your thinking as you do so. For example:

Dear Jack,
    Thank you for the invitation to your birthday party on Saturday 19 November.
    I will be able to come and I am looking forward to it.
Love from Jatinder

Consolidate the use of capital letters for the children's names and for days and months.
● Set up the role-play area for a tea party, with blank invitations, birthday cards and envelopes. Have an enlarged version of the party invitation available for the children to use to model their own writing if they wish. Allocate roles and ask the children to complete invitations or cards.
● Provide further opportunities for children to write their names using drawing and craft materials and sand and water to develop a kinaesthetic memory for the formation of their own names. Reinforce the convention of using a capital letter at the start.
● To design an invitation, recap on the various kinds of decoration that can be found on party invitations. Make a print block using polystyrene and print a border around a party invitation, or design invitations using ICT. Encourage the children to think about the decoration that suits a birthday party and the main words they need to include (*at, on,* the time and so on).

## Extension/further reading

Produce a postbag that contains an invitation from the chief teddy bear for every child and their favourite teddy to a teddy bear's tea party. Provide blank reply cards and ask the children to reply to the chief teddy, accepting his invitation.

Read *Kipper's Birthday* by Mick Inkpen (Hodder Children's Books) to reinforce the importance of putting the correct information on a party invitation.

R W6: to read on sight the 45 high-frequency words to be taught by the end of YR from Appendix List 1

R W8: to read and write own name

R S4: to use a capital letter for the start of own name

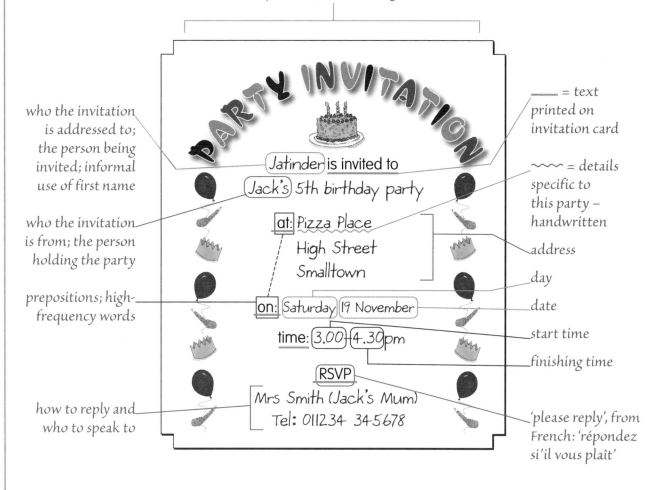

*clear layout; few words, only important information given*

PARTY INVITATION

Jatinder is invited to

Jack's 5th birthday party

at: Pizza Place
High Street
Smalltown

on: Saturday 19 November

time: 3.00 4.30pm

RSVP

Mrs Smith (Jack's Mum)
Tel: 01123 345678

*who the invitation is addressed to; the person being invited; informal use of first name*

*who the invitation is from; the person holding the party*

*prepositions; high-frequency words*

*how to reply and who to speak to*

*_____ = text printed on invitation card*

*~~~ = details specific to this party – handwritten*

*address*

*day*

*date*

*start time*

*finishing time*

*'please reply', from French: 'répondez si'il vous plaît'*

R T1: through shared reading:
● to recognise printed and handwritten words in a variety of settings, e.g. letters
● that words can be written down to be read again for a wide range of purposes

R T12: through guided and independent writing:
● to experiment with writing in a variety of play, exploratory and role-play situations
● to write their own names

R T15: to use writing to communicate in a variety of ways, incorporating it into play and everyday classroom life, e.g. letters

# Menu

## Background

Today, eating establishments from fast-food outlets to more upmarket restaurants provide special menus for children. Even some very young children are familiar with ordering their food from a menu that is set before them by pointing to the accompanying illustrations of the food. Children's menus frequently include colouring and puzzle activities to keep the children occupied during the meal.

The layout of a menu is basically a list, split into sections by sub-headings, a form of writing that many children will be familiar with from other contexts.

## Shared reading and discussing the text

● Gather together a range of children's menus from local restaurants and cafés and use them in a display.

● Ask the children about their experiences of eating in cafés and restaurants. Do they sometimes go out to eat? Does the place they go to have a special menu or special meals for children? What is different about an adult meal and children's meal? (For example, size of the portion, selection of food, inclusion of a toy, incentive for finishing the meal, price.) Do the menus offer the children's preferred meals?

● Have a look at the menu. Ask the children who would use it and where. Point out that it is organised in different sections (hot meals, cold meals, desserts and drinks).

● Read through the selection of hot meals and show how the prices are given. Demonstrate how to read down the list, but then across to see the corresponding price for each dish. Help the children to understand the £ and p notation and recognise the large numbers. Which of the hot meals would the children choose? Repeat for the choices of cold meals and desserts. Note that fruit is a generic term and could refer to bananas, apples and oranges, for instance. Conduct a quick survey of preferences.

● Ask the children to read the choice of drinks to you. Point out that you can choose a small drink or a large drink and that large drinks cost more than small ones. Ask the children to think of other words that could be used instead of *large*. (*Big, huge* or even *gigantic* or *enormous* for something that is extra large.)

## Activities

● Provide opportunities for children to write menus for the class café, using some pre-cut menu cards. They can choose their favourite meals and should be encouraged to think about some healthy options, such as including vegetables with a main meal, and fruit for dessert.

● Develop the idea of small and large portions to reinforce the concept of size differences and opposites. (This can be linked to 'Goldilocks and the three bears' on page 22.) Give the children a selection of objects and ask them to sort them into two hoops labelled *big* and *small*. Extend the activity by saying or writing words and asking the children to suggest opposites, for example *light* and *dark*, *thick* and *thin*, *night* and *day*, *tall* and *short*. Commercially produced matching-card games can be played to reinforce the concept of opposites.

● Together write a menu for a fairy tale character, such as the giant in 'Jack and the Beanstalk', Tom Thumb or Cinderella (at her wedding banquet). Before writing, talk about the sorts of things that the characters might like to eat and drink, and encourage the children to use their imaginations to invent meals. Help them to organise the meals into categories.

## Extension/further reading

Set up a café in the role-play area of the classroom. Include a range of menus and menu templates for children to produce their own. Provide notepads and pencils for waiters and waitresses. You could also create a kitchen area with utensils, weighing scales, cookery books and so on.

As well as the selection of children's menus, read books about food to reinforce healthy eating learning and Janet and Alan Ahlberg's *Mrs Wobble the Waitress* (Puffin Books).

R W5: to read on sight a range of familiar words

R W11: to make collections of personal interest or significant words and words linked to particular topics

R T1: through shared reading: that words can be written down to be read again for a wide range of purposes

several items listed that make up 1 dish

means 'small'; suitable for children

Italian words

food topic words

generic term

price

pounds

pence

opposites

encouragement to children to eat up their meals; also incentive to parents to buy the meal

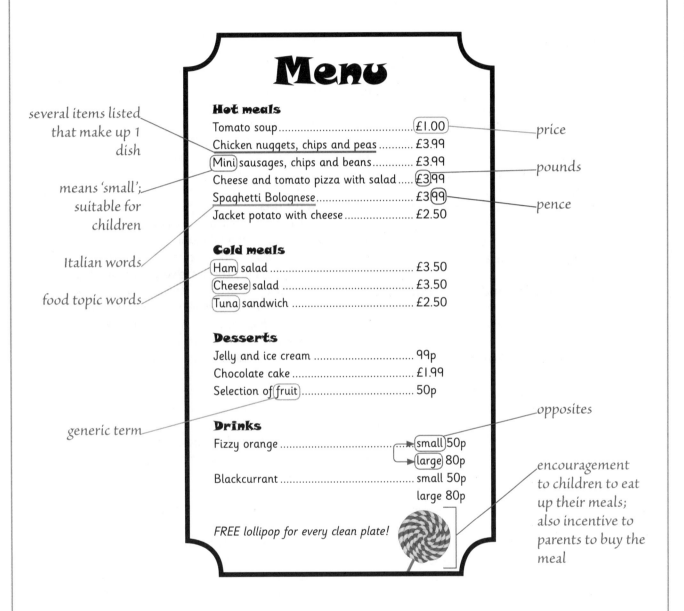

# Menu

**Hot meals**
Tomato soup ............................................. £1.00
Chicken nuggets, chips and peas ........... £3.99
Mini sausages, chips and beans ............. £3.99
Cheese and tomato pizza with salad ..... £3.99
Spaghetti Bolognese ............................... £3.99
Jacket potato with cheese ...................... £2.50

**Cold meals**
Ham salad ............................................... £3.50
Cheese salad .......................................... £3.50
Tuna sandwich ....................................... £2.50

**Desserts**
Jelly and ice cream ................................. 99p
Chocolate cake ....................................... £1.99
Selection of fruit .................................... 50p

**Drinks**
Fizzy orange ............................... small 50p
                                              large 80p
Blackcurrant .............................. small 50p
                                              large 80p

*FREE lollipop for every clean plate!*

R T12: to experiment with writing in a variety of play, exploratory and role-play situations

R T13: to think about what they intend to write, ahead of writing it

R T15: to use writing to communicate in a variety of ways, incorporating it into play and everyday classroom life, e.g. menus

# Cooking rules

## Background

These cooking rules outline some important rules of hygiene and safety that should be observed when cooking. Reading and discussing the rules provides an opportunity to consider why rules are necessary.

Rules, such as the school rules and rules/instructions for how to play games, usually take the form of an ordered list of steps, often numbered or bulleted. They are written for a specific audience and use direct address and imperative verbs.

This text is useful to re-read and display when looking at 'Chocolate apples' (page 36).

## Shared reading and discussing the text

● Organise a display of cooking equipment and utensils. Ask the children if they know what the items are used for.

● Talk with the children about their experiences of cooking. What have they made? Did they enjoy the experience? Were they successful? Did they help to clear up after the cooking? Ask them what rules we should observe when cooking, for example washing hands.

● Display the text and read it aloud to the children. Do the children recognise any of the rules from their cooking experiences?

● Ask *why* these rules exist. For example, why must you wash your hands? (So that you don't pick up germs or pass them on to anyone who might eat the food you are preparing.) Think about each of the rules in turn and then summarise the purpose of the rules: to tell us what and what not to do, and to give advice on safety and hygiene.

● Check that the children understand difficult vocabulary, such as *ingredients* and *equipment*.

● Point out the order the rules are written in and that they are numbered in order. Ask the children why the rules are in this order. Notice that some of the things need to be done before you start cooking, some are done during the cooking and the last one is done after the cooking has been completed.

● Briefly consider the layout of the rules. A line space is left between each rule to make it easier to read. The rules are numbered for quick reference as you are working through the steps. (It is easier to find rule 4 if it has the number 4 written next to it, otherwise you would have to count down from the top each time.) The point can be demonstrated by masking the numbers and then trying to locate a specific rule.

## Activities

● In role-play, tell the children that they are appearing on the television programme *Ready Steady Cook*. Explain that as the country's leading celebrity chefs it is very important that they follow the highest standards for hygiene and safety in the kitchen. As you relate events in the studio, the children should enact them. Incorporate the cooking rules into the drama.

● Ask the children to draw a picture showing one of the cooking rules that they think is especially important. Encourage the children to copy the rule as a caption for the picture and add labels if they can.

● Produce a set of picture cards depicting some of the rules (those that most obviously occur in a sequence). Ask pairs of children to talk about the rules that are shown on the cards and why those rules are important. They can then order the cards in the correct chronological sequence. Ask the children questions to prompt them to consider the appropriateness of the order they have selected. (*Would you need to wear oven gloves before measuring the ingredients?*)

● Consider what rules should be in place to make sure children play safely in the playground. In shared writing, compose a list of rules entitled *Playground Safety*. Alternatively, produce rules for a happy classroom.

## Extension/further reading

Books on this theme include *Stone Soup* by Tony Bonning and Sally Hobson (Gullane), *The Little Red Hen* by Jonathan Allen (Corgi) and Tony Blundell's version *Lucky Clucky* (Puffin).

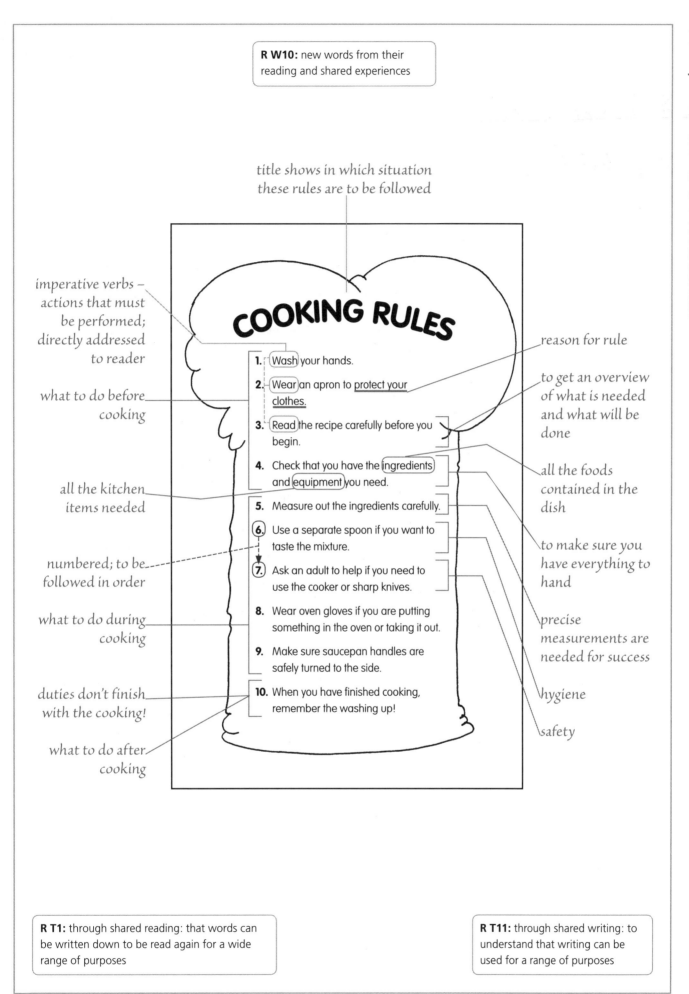

**R W10:** new words from their reading and shared experiences

title shows in which situation these rules are to be followed

# COOKING RULES

imperative verbs – actions that must be performed; directly addressed to reader

what to do before cooking

all the kitchen items needed

numbered; to be followed in order

what to do during cooking

duties don't finish with the cooking!

what to do after cooking

reason for rule

to get an overview of what is needed and what will be done

all the foods contained in the dish

to make sure you have everything to hand

precise measurements are needed for success

hygiene

safety

1. Wash your hands.
2. Wear an apron to protect your clothes.
3. Read the recipe carefully before you begin.
4. Check that you have the ingredients and equipment you need.
5. Measure out the ingredients carefully.
6. Use a separate spoon if you want to taste the mixture.
7. Ask an adult to help if you need to use the cooker or sharp knives.
8. Wear oven gloves if you are putting something in the oven or taking it out.
9. Make sure saucepan handles are safely turned to the side.
10. When you have finished cooking, remember the washing up!

**R T1:** through shared reading: that words can be written down to be read again for a wide range of purposes

**R T11:** through shared writing: to understand that writing can be used for a range of purposes

# Chocolate apples

### Background

This simple recipe can easily be followed and made by children, although adult help is required for the skewering of apples. It is an instructional text, including a bulleted list of what is needed (the ingredients and equipment) and, in this case, two sets of steps to be performed.

Like the list of cooking rules (see page 34), the text uses simple sentences with imperative verbs. It is organised in short sections with sub-headings and includes illustrations for clarity.

### Shared reading and discussing the text

● Gather a set of recipe books, including those specially produced for children, and make them available in the role-play area.

● Talk with the children about their knowledge of cooking. Ask whether they have seen cookery programmes on television, for example *Ready Steady Cook*. Mention some names of current popular celebrity chefs and see whether the children recognise any of them. Ask them if they have ever used a recipe or seen someone at home using one. What did they make? Was the recipe easy to follow?

● Show the children the recipe for chocolate apples. Read it through, drawing attention to the layout and the logical sequence of the steps. Notice the exclamation-mark icon indicating that this step needs care because it involves hot water.

● Ask the children if they know the meaning of *heatproof*. Explain that something that is heatproof can hold hot things and be heated without breaking. Ask the children if they know any other words ending in *-proof* (for example, *waterproof, showerproof, childproof, soundproof*) and clarify the meanings.

### Activities

● Make the chocolate apples. Display an enlarged copy of the recipe so that it can be referred to during the cookery session. Direct the children's attention to the recipe as you read out each step in the procedure.

● After making the recipe, encourage the children to talk about what they did to the rest of the class. Guide them to think about the logical sequence in the procedure. Encourage them to produce a recount in words or pictures, or a combination, of what they did.

● In shared writing, invent a recipe for a fairy tale character, such as Hansel or Gretel. Think about a dish the character would like and what size portion they would need. (This can be developed from the fairy tale menus activity on page 32.)

● Point out that if a recipe is to be successful the steps must be followed in the order they are written: you can't dip the apples in the chocolate before you have melted it and it would be really messy if you tried to do it before you had pushed the skewer into the apple! Produce a set of cards giving individual steps of the recipe – these could be pictures, text or a combination depending on the children's levels. In pairs, the children can use the cards to show the correct sequence for the recipe. Talk to the children about why they have put the cards in the order they have.

### Extension/further reading

Produce a big book of the children's favourite recipes. The recipe book can be referred to in shared reading and kept in the role-play café.

Good cookery books include *The Usborne First Cookbook* by Angela Wilkes and *Kids' First Cook Book* (Dorling Kindersley).

*title tells reader what dish recipe will make*

*step 1: preparation*

*quantities*

*long, thin pieces of wood to use as handles*

*step 2: start cooking*

*adverb tells reader how to heat the water*

*step 3: final touches*

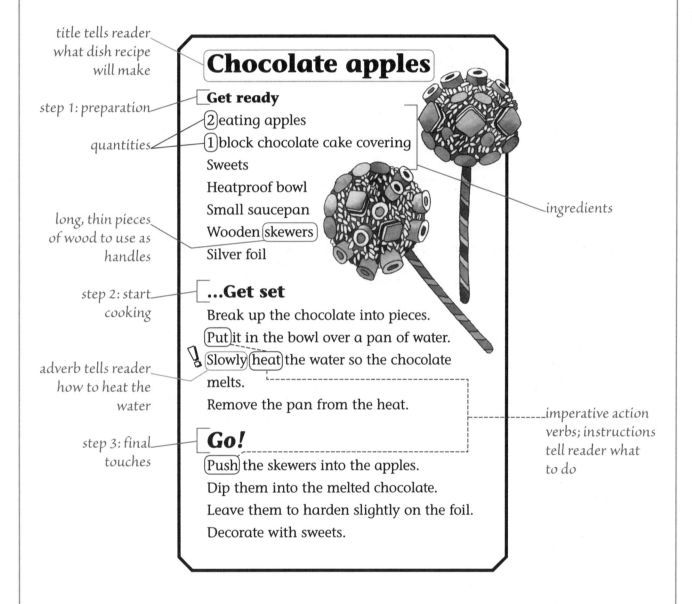

# Chocolate apples

**Get ready**

2 eating apples

1 block chocolate cake covering

Sweets

Heatproof bowl

Small saucepan

Wooden skewers

Silver foil

## ...Get set

Break up the chocolate into pieces.

Put it in the bowl over a pan of water.

Slowly heat the water so the chocolate melts.

Remove the pan from the heat.

## Go!

Push the skewers into the apples.

Dip them into the melted chocolate.

Leave them to harden slightly on the foil.

Decorate with sweets.

*ingredients*

*imperative action verbs; instructions tell reader what to do*

# Let's Look at Fruit

### Background

The descriptive non-fiction writing in *Let's Look at Fruit* provides a multi-sensory look at fruit and can be used as a model for encouraging children to record their observations of fruit in art and design. Some less familiar fruit are looked at in this extract. Children can be encouraged to consider the descriptive language of the text and to extend their vocabulary through engagement with multi-sensory observations. The children should consider how pictures add to the information provided by the text.

### Shared reading and discussing the text

● Gather a collection of fruit, including those mentioned in the text. Ask the children if they can name the fruit, and write these on the board. Pass the items of fruit around and ask the children to describe the texture of the skin and the smell of each fruit as well as the colours. Cut the fruit to look inside and ask the children to describe what each piece of fruit looks like. If appropriate, let the children taste little pieces of the fruit.

● Explain that you are going to read a text that describes different fruit. Read it through, then look at the pictures. Consider whether the pictures provide information that is not mentioned in the text, for example the shape, details in the pattern of seeds.

● Draw attention to the different words that are used to describe textures (*soft, squishy, prickly, juicy*).

● Pick out alliterative words from the text to develop the children's hearing of initial sounds. Look at the description of bananas as *soft and squishy*. Ask the children if they can hear which letter sound the words begin with. Together, make up a sentence with a few words beginning with *s*: *Sally saw a silly singing seal*.

● Write down as many names of fruit as the children can think of, and some that they may not know, and produce a display of topic words.

### Activities

● Assemble different collections of fruit and ask the children in groups to offer descriptions of the fruit. Cut the fruit and ask them to describe what it looks like on the inside. Take Polaroid or digital photographs of the whole and cut fruit. Repeat the activity with the groups looking at different fruit.

● Produce a class book of fruit. Show the children the photographs of the fruit. Discuss which they think are the clearest images and select the photographs they want to include in the book. Ask the children to label the photographs. As well as the names of the fruit as headings, these labels might include *skin, pips, seeds, flesh, stone* and *peel*. The book could be produced on the computer using a word-processing package and digital photographs.

● On pieces of card (one for each child), write the words *banana, pineapple, mango* and *orange*. Distribute the cards and ask the children to place their cards on their table in alphabetical order. Ask who has the word *banana*. (For children who need extra help, point to the word *banana* in the text.) Draw attention to the initial phoneme *b*. Go through the rest of the alphabet together, stopping when you come to *m, o* and *p* and ask the children to check the order of their cards.

● Make a feely box. Inside the box, place objects with different textures (slimy, soft, prickly, smooth, rough and so on). Ask the children to describe the texture and identify as many of the objects as they can.

### Extension/further reading

Provide a range of drawing and craft materials for children to use to make pictures of the fruit.

Read the rest of *Let's Look at Fruit* and compare the photographs and labels with the class book. Other multi-sensory books about food include *Scratch and Sniff Food* (Dorling Kindersley).

**R W3:** alphabetic and phonic knowledge through: understanding alphabetical order

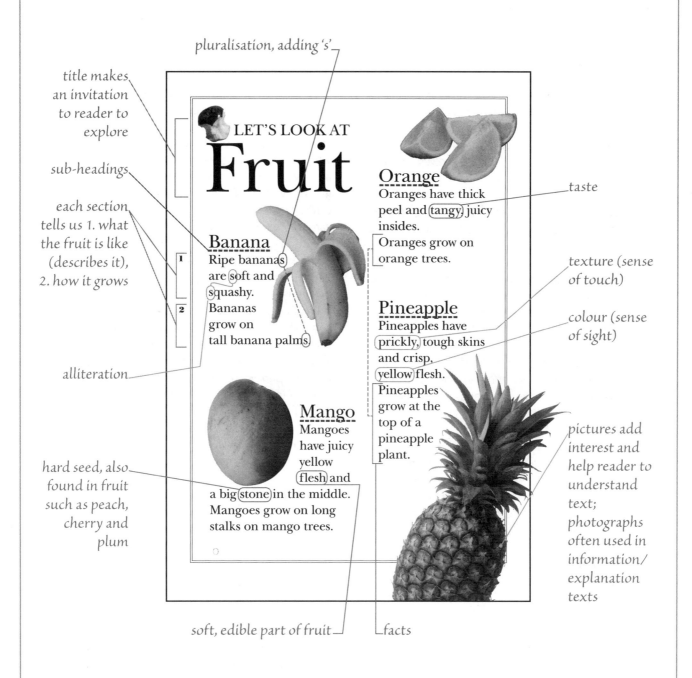

pluralisation, adding 's'

title makes an invitation to reader to explore

sub-headings

each section tells us 1. what the fruit is like (describes it), 2. how it grows

alliteration

hard seed, also found in fruit such as peach, cherry and plum

### LET'S LOOK AT
# Fruit

#### Banana
Ripe bananas are soft and squashy. Bananas grow on tall banana palms.

#### Mango
Mangoes have juicy yellow flesh and a big stone in the middle. Mangoes grow on long stalks on mango trees.

#### Orange
Oranges have thick peel and tangy, juicy insides. Oranges grow on orange trees.

#### Pineapple
Pineapples have prickly, tough skins and crisp, yellow flesh. Pineapples grow at the top of a pineapple plant.

taste

texture (sense of touch)

colour (sense of sight)

pictures add interest and help reader to understand text; photographs often used in information/ explanation texts

soft, edible part of fruit

facts

**R W11:** to make collections of personal interest or significant words linked to particular topics

**R T12:** through guided and independent writing: to write labels or captions for pictures and drawings

# My body

## Background

This simple diagram presents key topic vocabulary in a familiar context and introduces writing for different purposes. An important aspect of labelling is clear signing so that it is obvious what the label is attached to. Children could label drawings of themselves or label objects in the classroom.

## Shared reading and discussing the text

● Prepare the text by masking the labels. Share the diagram with the children, asking them to name the different body parts. Take the mask off each label in turn, drawing attention to the structure of the words.

● Draw attention to the way the labels are written with a line clearly showing which parts they refer to.

● Discuss similarities and differences between children (such as hair and eye colour). Encourage respect for difference and recognition of universally human characteristics.

## Activities

● Laminate an enlarged version of the text with a set of label cards and make these available for the children to incorporate in their play. You might also have a copy of the text available to encourage word matching for children requiring support with this activity.

● Work with a small group to take digital photographs of each other. Print the photographs and label the parts of the body, using the diagram for reference. In shared writing, extend this by composing descriptive sentences, for example *Ravi has brown hair. Rachel has red hair. Max has blue eyes. Sita has brown eyes.* Produce a class book incorporating the labelled photographs and the sentences.

● Mask the labels on the text before copying it for groups. Tell the children that the labels have been jumbled up and you need their help to put them back again. Hand out a set of label cards to each group. Point to different parts of the pictures and ask the children to name that part. Ask the child who has the correct label to attach it to their diagram. Encourage the children to check with their group members whether it is the correct word. Repeat the activity for other parts of the body.

● Play a version of 'Simon Says' using the label cards: *Simple Simon says touch your...* (show card for *head*).

● Provide some outline drawings of animals and ask the children to label them with body parts. List some additional vocabulary that may be needed, such as *tail, whiskers* and so on.

● In shared writing, further develop the concept of labelling. Produce labels for classroom objects, drawing attention to the structure of words as you write them, for example *pencils, scissors, paper, glue.* Ask the children to attach the labels to the objects they belong to. Alternatively, provide a collection of objects and ask the children to sort them into the correct containers using labels to help them.

## Extension/further reading

Make a simple zigzag book entitled *Let's Look at Eyes.* Gather a collection of human and animal eye pictures from magazines, catalogues, brochures and so on. Paste an eye picture on each page of the zigzag book. On the first page, write the question, *Who do these eyes belong to?* Similar books can be made of ears and hair/fur.

Develop children's existing knowledge about the human body. Encourage them to ask questions and use a range of resources to help them find answers.

Look at other non-fiction books that have labelled diagrams, for example Lola Schaeffer's *It's My Body* Big Book compilation (Raintree).

**R T1:** to recognise printed and handwritten words in a variety of settings, e.g. labels

**R W11:** to make collections of personal interest or significant words and words linked to particular topics

**R W5:** to read on sight a range of familiar words, e.g. captions, labels

**R T12:** through guided and independent writing:
- to experiment with writing in a variety of play, exploratory and role-play situations
- to write labels or captions for pictures and drawings

**R T15:** to use writing to communicate in a variety of ways, incorporating it into play and everyday classroom life, e.g. labels

simple diagram

one-word label for each major body part

lines show which word labels which body part

# My body

head

neck

fingers

back

leg

shoulder

hand

arm

knee

ankle

foot

toes

title tells reader what topic text will give information about

human bodies all essentially the same

# Wet World

by Norma Simon

## Background

This extract is one of several texts on aspects of the weather. The story has strong alliterative qualities and an interesting emphasis on wet throughout the story until the very end, where the dry child inside the wet clothes and wet world provides a satisfying conclusion.

## Shared reading and discussing the text

● Display a collection of wet weather clothes and accessories (boots, raincoat, umbrella).

● Talk about rainy days with the children. What do they do in the rain? (For example, jump in puddles, follow raindrops on the windows.) Do they like to be inside or outside when it is raining? What do they dislike about rainy days? (Perhaps not being allowed out at playtime, being splashed by cars.)

● Read the poem, then discuss favourite lines. Talk about wet and dry as opposites.

● Ask the children if they have special clothes for when it is raining. Establish that we wear these clothes to keep us dry.

● Some words in the extract describe the sounds that can be heard on rainy days: *Windscreen wipers wipe the wet*; *swish*; and *whish*. Practise making the movement of the wipers and mimicking the sound they make. What other sounds does rain make? For example, rain on a window: *pitter-patter*. Practise mimicking the sounds and use light finger tapping to accompany the pitter-patter.

● Re-read the last three lines of the first section, emphasising the alliteration. Ask the children if they notice anything special about the words. Develop this into a game of odd one out: say a list of words and ask the children to put their hands up if they hear a word that does not belong to the *w* list (for example, *wheels, whistle, water, mum, washing*).

## Activities

● Write down the two lines beginning *Windscreen wipers*. Re-read the lines together, practising the actions made by the windscreen wipers. Remind the children of other words that described the different sounds made by rain and write another sentence for the poem using one of these sounds. For example, *Raindrops splash into the puddles / Plip-plop plip-plop*. This can be repeated for other sounds, such as *pitter-patter* and *swish-swash*.

● Put the lines together to make a class poem. Display this in the role-play area where the children can practise reading it.

● Involve the children in writing labels for the wet-weather clothing display. As you write the labels, draw attention to how the words are constructed, for example the number of phonemes they can identify in each word, initial phonemes, final phonemes.

● Collect words that rhyme with *wet* and add these to the display.

● Use sound words as the basis of a dance lesson. *Whish-whish* could generate swaying movements; *pitter-patter* light running; *plip-pop* jumping softly on the spot. Construct a rainy day story that the children accompany with a sequence of movements. Use a digital camera to take photographs. Follow up the dance session by writing captions for the photographs in shared writing. Display the photographs and captions.

● Sit the children in a circle and give each child an object. Place two hoops in the centre of the circle. Recap the initial phoneme in *wet*. In turn, ask the children if they have an object that starts with the same letter. The children should then place their objects in the *w* hoop or the *not w* hoop. At the end of the activity say the words of all of the items in the *w* hoop. These can then be written on a large sheet of paper and displayed with the items. A few questions can be written on cards to accompany the display: *Can you find the watch? Can you find the wheel? Can you find the watering can?*

## Extension/further reading

Other books include *Alfie Weather* by Shirley Hughes (Red Fox), *Pete's Puddles* by Hannah Roche and Pierre Pratt (Zero to Ten) and *Rain and Us* by Jillian Powell (Belitha Press).

# WET WORLD

*Extract 1*

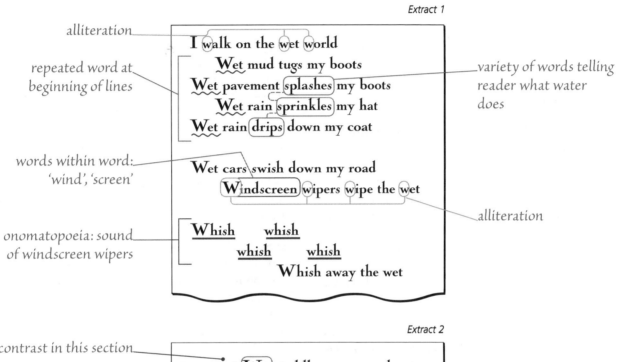

alliteration

repeated word at beginning of lines

variety of words telling reader what water does

words within word: 'wind', 'screen'

alliteration

onomatopoeia: sound of windscreen wipers

*Extract 2*

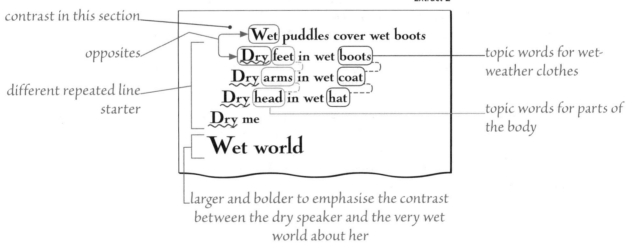

contrast in this section

opposites

different repeated line starter

topic words for wet-weather clothes

topic words for parts of the body

larger and bolder to emphasise the contrast between the dry speaker and the very wet world about her

# A Summery Saturday Morning

by Margaret Mahy

## Background

This rhyming story with a refrain provides a supportive structure for beginning readers. The playful romp is set during a walk and the text includes clues that suggest a seashore setting. Journey stories such as this one provide an excellent opportunity for group drawing. The story can be sung to the tune of 'Here We Go Round the Mulberry Bush'.

## Shared reading and discussing the text

● Make available a selection of pictures that relate to the story setting (sand dunes, beach, mudflats) or if you live close to a similar setting visit it with the class before reading the text.

● Draw on the children's experiences. Do any of them have pet dogs? Do they have any stories about adventures they have had when taking their dogs for a walk?

● Explain that this story is about what happens when two dogs meet some geese. Ask them if they can guess what will happen.

● Read the text aloud, emphasising the changes in mood and pace. (The walk starts at a leisurely pace but speeds up as the dogs chase the geese and then the geese chase the dogs.)

● Ask the children if anything happened in the story that they expected. Did anything happen that they did not expect?

● Re-read the text together, pausing before the rhyme at the end of the third line to allow the children to supply the rhyming word. Draw attention to the visual similarities between rhyming words where appropriate (such as *track/black*; *away/play*).

## Activities

● In shared writing, compose a story about an eventful walk. This could be a walk to school, to the shops or in the country.

● On large sheets of paper, ask small groups of children to draw the story. If preferred, some landmarks (a path, sand dunes, beach) can be outlined on the paper as part of a guided reading activity and the children can draw the details independently. Ask the children to tell you about their drawing and share it with other children in the class. Observing group drawing provides an excellent opportunity for assessing response to, and comprehension of, the text.

● Create a story box to stimulate the children's imaginative play. The box can include an outline map or play mat; model geese, dogs and people. Make an enlarged copy of the text available in the play area.

● In a small group, ask the children to create two freeze frames, one before the arrival of the geese and one after. Help the children by asking questions. What might the children be doing on the walk? (Playing with a beach ball, eating an ice cream, picking things up and looking at them and so on.) Ask one of the children to take on the role of family photographer to take the picture. The children can take on the role of any family member, but not dogs or geese. If a digital camera is available, actual photographs can be taken; if not, using a photographer as a dramatic device helps young children develop still images by creating a concrete context.

● Read the line *The geese turn round and flap and hiss*. Geese are noted for their aggressive hissing. What sounds do other birds make? Ask if anyone knows the sound made by a mute swan. (It doesn't make a sound, except just before it dies, hence the saying 'swan song'.) Play a recording of bird sounds for the children to listen to. They can identify the birds and practise mimicking them.

## Extension/further reading

Make a wall story using the children's artwork and incorporating key lines from the text.

Other journey stories include *We're Going on a Bear Hunt* by Michael Rosen and Helen Oxenbury (Walker Books), *We're Going on a Lion Hunt* by David Axtell (Macmillan), *Rosie's Walk* by Pat Hutchins (Puffin) and *Each Peach Pear Plum* by Janet and Allan Ahlberg (Puffin). Margaret Mahy has written some great stories for young children. Her recent collections include *Wonderful Me* and *Wait for Me* (both Orion).

**R W1:** to understand and be able to rhyme through: recognising, exploring and working with rhyming patterns

**R W9:** to recognise the critical features of words, e.g. shape, length, and common spelling patterns

alliterative title

describes the track

appropriate setting for country walk

more information on setting: knotted long grass or other foliage

signals trouble!

smooth and glossy

satisfying bouncy rhythm

topic link to other days of the week; initial capital letter

'-ack' rhyme family; others include:
  back
  sack
  stack

'-een' rhyme family; others include:
  seen
  bean
  clean

indicates fast, dynamic movement; gives hints about setting: suggests a beach

characteristic of geese

more detail on setting

movement and noise; geese notoriously aggressive

italicised for emphasis

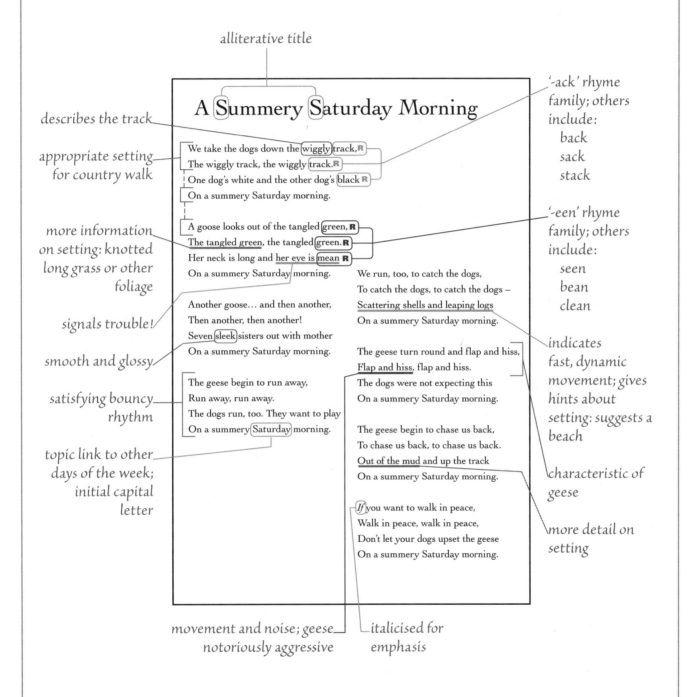

# A Summery Saturday Morning

We take the dogs down the wiggly track, **R**
The wiggly track, the wiggly track. **R**
One dog's white and the other dog's black **R**
On a summery Saturday morning.

A goose looks out of the tangled green, **R**
The tangled green, the tangled green. **R**
Her neck is long and her eye is mean **R**
On a summery Saturday morning.

Another goose… and then another,
Then another, then another!
Seven sleek sisters out with mother
On a summery Saturday morning.

The geese begin to run away,
Run away, run away.
The dogs run, too. They want to play
On a summery Saturday morning.

We run, too, to catch the dogs,
To catch the dogs, to catch the dogs –
Scattering shells and leaping logs
On a summery Saturday morning.

The geese turn round and flap and hiss,
Flap and hiss, flap and hiss.
The dogs were not expecting this
On a summery Saturday morning.

The geese begin to chase us back,
To chase us back, to chase us back.
Out of the mud and up the track
On a summery Saturday morning.

*If* you want to walk in peace,
Walk in peace, walk in peace,
Don't let your dogs upset the geese
On a summery Saturday morning.

**R T2:** to use a variety of cues when reading: knowledge of the story and its context, and awareness of how it should make sense grammatically

**R T8:** to locate and read significant parts of the text, e.g. names of key characters, rhymes and chants

# Five Ducks Five

by Sarah Hayes

## Background

This extract is from a longer rhyming story – *Nine Ducks Nine*, which makes use of a traditional countdown structure. As the fox approaches the group of ducks, they disappear one by one to the rickety bridge. Are the clever ducks setting a trap for the fox, or is his final comeuppance just a lucky escape for the remaining duck? (A similar device is used in *Rosie's Walk* by Pat Hutchins.) The text features repetition and rhymes within lines.

The counting element can be used to link to 'Monsters' (page 58).

## Shared reading and discussing the text

● Ask the children to share any counting rhymes they know, particularly those they have learned at home and rhymes in languages other than English.
● Show the extract and read it together.
● Ask the children if they know what *rickety* means and define it for them if necessary.
● Show the children that the extract can be followed like a counting game. Start with five fingers out and fold one down each time a duck leaves.
● Ask the children whether they think the ducks knew that the rickety bridge would collapse and led the fox there on purpose. (The end of the book suggests they did.)
● Draw attention to the bold, enlarged letters in the line *Mr Fox Pounced!* Ask how this line should be read. Notice the ellipsis on the previous line, which is used to build suspense before the fox pounces. Ask one of the children to read the two lines, demonstrating the suspense and surprise. Practise reading these lines together.

## Activities

● Explain that in the full story there are nine ducks rather than five. Write a verse in shared writing for 'six ducks six'. Three lines of each stanza remain basically the same; it is only the first line that requires significant rewriting. Remind the children that the first line includes an internal rhyme. Generate a list of rhyming words for *six* (such as *fix, mix, bricks, chicks, licks, tricks*) then write the verse:

> Six Ducks *Six* were up to their *tricks.*
> Mr Fox came closer.
> One duck flew away,
> down to the rickety bridge.

This activity could be repeated with different groups for numbers seven to nine. Re-read the extract, adding the new verses.
● Help the children to perform the poem in groups of five (or more if you have narrators).
● Retell the extract as a circle story, embellishing the details. Tell the children the beginning of the story, demonstrating how to add to it, for example with adjectives describing the fox or the ducks, then pass it on to the child sitting to your left. You might want to use an object (such as a plastic duck) to pass around to signal who is telling the next part of the story.
● As a circle game, generate new rhymes, real and invented, for each of the rhyming pairs in the poem (for example, *five/dive: live, hive, thrive*). See how many different rhymes the children can suggest for each pair.
● Produce a set of snap cards with simple illustrations of nine ducks, eight ducks and so on. Write *nine, eight...* at the bottom of each card. When a snap is made, draw attention to the word on the card and its spelling.

## Extension/further reading

Books of rhymes include *One, Two, Skip a Few* (Barefoot Books), *Nonsense Counting Rhymes* by Kaye Umansky and Chris Fisher (OUP), *A Caribbean Counting Book* by Faustin Charles and Roberta Arenson (Barefoot Books). Books that feature dramatic irony include *Rosie's Walk* by Pat Hutchins (Red Fox) and *Handa's Surprise* by Eileen Browne (Walker Books).

**R W1:** to understand and be able to rhyme through:
● recognising, exploring and working with rhyming patterns
● extending these patterns by analogy, generating new and invented words in speech and spelling

**R W11:** to make collections of words linked to particular topics

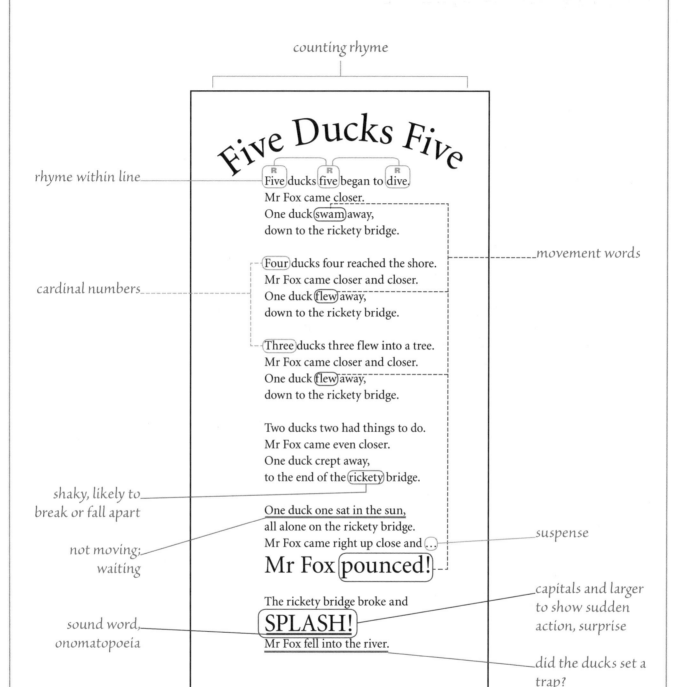

counting rhyme

## Five Ducks Five

rhyme within line

Five ducks five began to dive.
Mr Fox came closer.
One duck swam away,
down to the rickety bridge.

Four ducks four reached the shore.
Mr Fox came closer and closer.
One duck flew away,
down to the rickety bridge.

Three ducks three flew into a tree.
Mr Fox came closer and closer.
One duck flew away,
down to the rickety bridge.

Two ducks two had things to do.
Mr Fox came even closer.
One duck crept away,
to the end of the rickety bridge.

One duck one sat in the sun,
all alone on the rickety bridge.
Mr Fox came right up close and ...
Mr Fox pounced!

The rickety bridge broke and
SPLASH!
Mr Fox fell into the river.

movement words

cardinal numbers

shaky, likely to break or fall apart

not moving; waiting

suspense

capitals and larger to show sudden action, surprise

did the ducks set a trap?

sound word, onomatopoeia

**R T7:** to use knowledge of familiar texts to re-enact or retell to others, recounting the main points in correct sequence

**R T9:** to be aware of story structures, e.g. actions/reactions, consequences, and the ways that stories are built up and concluded

**R T10:** to re-read and recite stories and rhymes with predictable and repeated patterns and experiment with similar rhyming patterns

# Wolf's diary

by Nikki Gamble

## Background

This text reinforces children's recognition of the days of the week and knowledge of their order, and introduces them to dates within a month. It can help to illustrate the differences between handwritten and printed text. This diary is a record of each day, written after the event, rather than an appointments diary which looks forward and reminds us of important dates coming up. It uses recognisable fairy tale characters and typical weekly events.

You might want to link this text to work on 'A Week at Gran's' (page 56).

## Shared reading and discussing the text

● Prior to reading the text, provide an example of a diary to show the children, ideally both completed and blank pages. Ask if any of them have a diary or know anyone who has one. Ask if they know what diaries are for. Sometimes people keep a diary to remind them of the things they need to do. Sometimes people keep a diary to record what they have done so they will be able to read it later and remember interesting events.

● Show the children the page from Wolf's diary. Point out that some of the page is written in typed print and some of it in handwriting script. Looking at the other diary example too, show the children that the dates are pre-printed and the diary owner (Wolf) has handwritten the entries for each day. Notice that this page covers a whole week.

● Read the diary to discover what Wolf has been doing. After reading, ask the children what kind of character they think Wolf is. Encourage them to support what they think by referring to the text. (For example, *He is playful because he is always wanting somebody to play with*; *he is very fond of food* – this is mentioned every day and with emphasis; *he seems to be quite lonely at the beginning when the little pigs do not want to play with him; he is enthusiastic and excitable.*)

● Ask the children why some of the words are in capital letters. Do they notice the exclamation marks too? How should these words be read? (Loudly and with enthusiasm to demonstrate how Wolf was feeling.)

## Activities

● Produce a class diary recording daily activities and events in class or school. Start it off by asking the children to recall significant events from the day before or today. Demonstrate how to write about them briefly in the space for the appropriate date. The diary could be reproduced in a newsletter that the children could share with adults at home. Alternatively, the diary page can be incorporated into the school or class web page and regularly updated with help from the children.

● Ask the children to make individual diary entries with a written or pictorial record of the day's favourite activity.

● Produce a set of cards of the days of the week for a box or folder. Show them to the children and as you read them together, draw attention to the structure of the words, for example the word-within-a-word *day* that ends each day's name. Display a sentence starter like *Today is* \_\_\_\_\_, and ask one of the children each day to find the correct word for the day.

● Include copies of blank diary pages, old diaries, calendars and story books that use diaries in the writing or imaginative play area, so that children are encouraged to include diary writing in their role-play repertoire.

## Extension/further reading

Read one of Philippe Dupasquier's *Busy Day* books (Walker Books) and use the structure as a model for a class book, *A Busy Day in Class*.

*Mr Wolf's Week* by Colin Hawkins (Egmont) is a day-by-day story; other suggested titles are *Arthur and the Lost Diary* by Marc Brown (Red Fox) and *Good Days Bad Days* by Catherine and Laurence Anholt (Orchard).

**R W5:** to read on sight a range of familiar words

**R T1:** through shared reading:
● to recognise printed and handwritten words in a variety of settings
● that words can be written down to be read again for a wide range of purposes

book to fill in with reminders of important dates coming up or to complete with what you have done each day

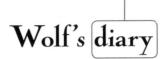

## Wolf's diary

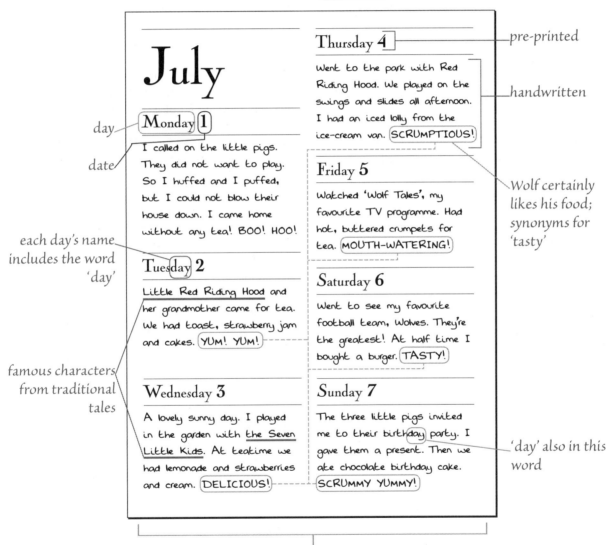

pre-printed

handwritten

Wolf certainly likes his food; synonyms for 'tasty'

day

date

each day's name includes the word 'day'

famous characters from traditional tales

'day' also in this word

this diary page covers whole week

### July

**Monday 1**

I called on the little pigs. They did not want to play. So I huffed and I puffed, but I could not blow their house down. I came home without any tea! BOO! HOO!

**Tuesday 2**

Little Red Riding Hood and her grandmother came for tea. We had toast, strawberry jam and cakes. YUM! YUM!

**Wednesday 3**

A lovely sunny day. I played in the garden with the Seven Little Kids. At teatime we had lemonade and strawberries and cream. DELICIOUS!

**Thursday 4**

Went to the park with Red Riding Hood. We played on the swings and slides all afternoon. I had an iced lolly from the ice-cream van. SCRUMPTIOUS!

**Friday 5**

Watched 'Wolf Tales', my favourite TV programme. Had hot, buttered crumpets for tea. MOUTH-WATERING!

**Saturday 6**

Went to see my favourite football team, Wolves. They're the greatest! At half time I bought a burger. TASTY!

**Sunday 7**

The three little pigs invited me to their birthday party. I gave them a present. Then we ate chocolate birthday cake. SCRUMMY YUMMY!

**R T11:** through shared writing: to understand that writing can be used for a range of purposes

**R T12:** through guided and independent writing: to experiment with writing in a variety of play, exploratory and role-play situations

**R T15:** to use writing to communicate in a variety of ways, incorporating it into play and everyday classroom life, e.g. recounting their own experiences, lists, labels

# I hear thunder Traditional

## Background

This is a popular song with a very familiar tune – it can be sung as a round to the tune of 'Frere Jacques'. The text can also be sung or read with accompanying actions. The repeated lines support prediction and encourage word-for-word matching.

## Shared reading and discussing the text

● Read or sing the rhyme, following the words with a pointer.
● Ask the children if they notice a pattern to the song. Draw attention to the repeated lines.
● Teach actions for the song, for example:

*I hear thunder* (put hand to ear)
*Oh! don't you?* (point to other children)
*Pitter, patter raindrops* (make rain falling action with fingers)
*I'm wet through* (hug self)
*I see blue skies* (put hand to eyes)
*Way up high* (point or reach to sky)
*Hurry up the sunshine* (make a circle with hands to indicate sunshine)
*I'll soon dry* (shake arms as if shaking water from them).

Alternatively, ask the children for suggestions for new actions.
● Instead of miming actions, clap the rhythm as you sing or chant. Then ask the children to clap without singing – hearing the song in their heads. Some children will find this challenging; it is more demanding than clapping and singing at the same time.
● Ask the children to suggest other songs and rhymes that they know about the weather, for example 'Dr Foster Went to Gloucester', 'The North Wind Doth Blow', 'Rain Rain Go Away'. Recite the rhymes together.

## Activities

● Ask the children to draw a stormy or a sunny day. Display the stormy pictures with the first verse of the poem and the sunny pictures with the second verse.

● As you sing the song again, ask the children in groups to mime a day at the seaside. Tell them to imagine that it is a nice sunny day at the beach. What sorts of things might they be doing? (Making sandcastles, playing in the sea, eating ice cream.) Then they hear thunder – a storm is coming – what will they do now? (Quickly pack everything away, head for shelter.) They feel the first raindrops. (Perhaps they put their hands out to feel the rain or put umbrellas up as they head for shelter.) The rain eases and they see sunshine. (They return to the beach.) Freeze the action at key points and encourage the children to look at each other's poses.
● Write lines of the song on strips of card (that can be attached to a magnetic board or with Blu-Tack). Seat the children in a circle and distribute one set of the lines, retaining one set. Explain that you only have half of the song and they must help you find the other half so you can sing it together. Show and read the first line. Ask who has the matching line. Draw attention to features of the language as you go through the song: the number of words in a line, question marks, initial letters and so on. When the song is completed, sing it together and thank the children for helping you put it back together again.
● Tell the children that sometimes words hide within other words. Write the word *raindrop* and ask if anyone can see a word hiding inside it. Ask them to show you where the word is (*rain* or *drop*). Repeat this with *sunshine*.
● Make a book of favourite weather rhymes and ask the children to illustrate them or make collages of pictures from magazines.

## Extension/further reading

Make a video recording of the children singing the song with actions. Play it back and encourage the children to identify what they liked about their performance.

A good collection of poems is *Poems About Weather* compiled by Amanda Earl (Hodder Children's Books).

**R W5:** to read on sight a range of familiar words

**R T6:** to re-read frequently a variety of familiar texts

*structure of before, during and after brief thunderstorm*

*senses: hearing*

*patterned structure of repetition*

*question*

*alliteration, onomatopoeia*

# I hear thunder

I *hear* thunder,
I hear *thunder,*
Oh! don't you?
Oh! don't you?
Pitter, patter raindrops.
Pitter, patter raindrops.
I'm wet through.
I'm wet through

I *see* blue skies. A
I see blue skies. A
Way up high. B
Way up high. B
Hurry up the sunshine. C
Hurry up the sunshine. C
I'll soon dry. D
I'll soon dry. D

*Traditional*

□ = *weather topic words*

*words within word: 'rain', 'drops'*

*senses: sight*

*rhyme*

*words within word: 'sun', 'shine'*

*contrast between wet and dry*

**R T7:** to use knowledge of familiar texts to re-enact or retell to others, recounting the main points in correct sequence

**R T10:** to re-read and recite stories and rhymes with predictable and repeated patterns

# I Do Not Mind You, Winter Wind
by Jack Prelutsky

## Background
This poem is in the form of a polite complaint addressed directly to the wind. It has a gentle rhythm and predictable rhyme scheme. The tone is light-hearted and playful and the poem beautifully depicts the capricious nature and strength of the wind. There is some difficult vocabulary, but children will identify with the different sensations felt and the change from delicate tickling to forceful bowling over.

## Shared reading and discussing the text
● Display pictures depicting windy weather.
● Briefly talk about windy weather. Ask the children what kinds of things they can do on windy days, such as fly a kite, dry the washing outside. Conversely, talk about problems that can be caused by strong wind. (Hats get blown away, trees can be blown over in very strong winds, roof tiles come off, litter is blown about.)
● Read the poem and help the children to appreciate that the person speaking the lines is talking directly to the wind – the wind is being personified. Notice that *Winter Wind* has capital letters, as though it is the wind's name.
● What sorts of things doesn't this person mind about the wind? (Being tickled with snowflakes or feeling the wind nibble at his skin.) Ask the children why this person doesn't mind these things. Do they feel nice? But what does this person mind? Ask why he minds being knocked over. How would the last verse be spoken? Perhaps gradually getting louder, the last two lines slowly to emphasise how cross he is. Let pairs of children practise reading the last verse or last two lines to each other.
● Mention that the person speaking the poem seems to imagine that the wind is like a person that they can talk to.
● Encourage the children to recall the different words that describe what the wind does and the effects it causes (*whirling, tickling, nibble, scrambling* and so on). Re-read the poem and together work out what these words mean.
● Re-read the poem again, pausing to allow the children to predict the rhyming words.

## Activities
● Ask the children to draw a familiar scene, such as a park, garden, school playground, on a windy day. Share the pictures in a plenary session. Choose one picture and model writing a sentence about it. Scribe the children's suggestions on what to say, talking about how you are writing: where to start, the letters that words begin with and so on.
● Make letter fans (cards joined at one end with a flexible paper fastener) that include the initial phonemes of *rain, wind* and *snow,* among others, and hand these out to pairs of children. Collect objects beginning with the phonemes *r, w* and *s* in a bag. Place three hoops on the floor and put a picture of one of the weather types inside each hoop. Now take an object from the bag. Ask the children to find the fan card with the letter that matches the initial letter of the object. Then ask the children which hoop you should place the object in.
● Re-read the second verse and look at the *-in* rhyming family in *skin* and *in.* Encourage the children to think of other words from this rhyming family, for example *win, grin, thin, penguin, robin.* Link these to the weather topic where possible.
● In shared writing, write a list poem about a windy day, perhaps building on the sentence written earlier about one of the children's pictures. Encourage the children to recall things that they have seen or have happened to them on windy days. Read the poem back to the children, then display it where they can practise reading it.

## Extension/further reading
Play the game 'A Day Out at the Park' at www.funwithspot.com, matching activities to different kinds of weather.

Read *The Wind Blew* by Pat Hutchins (Red Fox), *It's Windy* by Ed Vere (Macmillan Children's Books) or *Windy* by Robin Mitchell (Simply Read Books). Non-fiction books include *Wind* by Monique Felix (The Creative Company) and *Wind and Us* by Jillian Powell (Belitha Press).

**R W1:** to understand and be able to rhyme through: recognising, exploring and working with rhyming patterns

**R W4:** to link sound and spelling patterns by: using knowledge of rhyme to identify families of rhyming words

**R W10:** new words from their reading and shared experiences

# I Do Not Mind You, Winter Wind

direct address to the wind as a person

1st person speaker of poem

verbs tell what the wind does and effects it causes; wind shown to behave like a person or animal

moving hurriedly

trying

pause for emphasis and effect: speaker is quite cross!

capital letters for the wind's name

words within word: 'snow', 'flakes'

alternate lines rhyme

knock, tumble

alliteration

I do not mind you, Winter Wind
when you come whirling by,
to tickle me with snowflakes
drifting softly from the sky.

I do not even mind you
when you nibble at my skin,
scrambling over all of me
attempting to get in.

But when you bowl me over
and I land on my behind,
then I must tell you, Winter Wind,
I mind… I really mind!

*Jack Prelutsky*

**R S3:** that words are ordered left to right and need to be read that way to make sense

**R T3:** to re-read a text to provide context cues to help read unfamiliar words

**R T11:** through shared writing: to understand how letters are formed and used to spell words

# The Bad Day ABC by Hilda Offen

## Background

This extract is from the beginning of Hilda Offen's alphabet book, *The Bad Day ABC*. The text can be used to reinforce knowledge of alphabetic order and, in being highly alliterative, also develop phonological awareness. Any of the initial phonemes can be the focus of specific phonic teaching. The extract can provide a stimulus for a class thematic alphabet book (such as children's names, animals, food). The bizarre, humorous images in this text lend themselves to interpretation through art.

## Shared reading and discussing the text

● Prior to reading the text, practise reciting the alphabet or singing an alphabet song.
● Read the extract. Ask the children why it is a *bad day ABC*. (Everything is going wrong.)
● Ask the children which lines they thought were the funniest or most appealing. Why?
● Re-read the text, stopping after each line to ask if any of the children have a name that begins with the same letter. Write the names and draw attention to the initial capital letter.
● To develop phonological awareness, re-read each line, emphasising the alliteration. Ask if they can hear the initial sound in, for example, *bear* in line 2. Ask if any other words in the line start in the same way as *bear*.

## Activities

● Work with a small group to add further lines to the text (for example, ibex, jellyfish, kangaroo). Allocate sets of letters to different groups and complete the poem to z (you might have to leave out x!), then make it into a book. The children could choose a favourite line and draw an illustration to accompany it. Read the book in shared reading and make it available for the children to read independently. A variation of the activity is to produce semi-completed lines and ask the children which object should be added to complete the lines. (For example, *An irate ibex ate an*: orange, ice cream, apple; *A jellyfish juggled*: peas, sausages, jigsaw pieces).

● Play an initial phoneme game. Give each child a card with a letter of the alphabet and check that they know the 'sound' made by their letter. Practise the alphabet by asking the children to call out their letters in alphabetical order. Using a set of picture cards, show the cards one at a time and ask the children to hold up their card if it matches the beginning sound of the object in the picture. Together, make up silly alliterative sentences about the objects, for example *A bear bought a blue banana*. As you write, draw attention to individual letters making up the word and the direction you are writing in. Stress the initial letters of the alliterative words. A variation for children with less letter experience is to play the game by allocating children the initial letter of their own names.
● Briefly consider why we sometimes arrange names in alphabetical order, for example for the register, in a directory. Alphabetical order helps us to find things quickly. Space out one set of letter cards on the floor in alphabetical order. Hold up each card from a second set in turn and ask whether anyone has a name beginning with the letter. Tell the children to go and stand by their letter in the alphabet line. When the children are arranged alphabetically, ask them to look at who comes before them and who comes after. Next, ask the children to scatter around the room, then, on your signal, calmly arrange themselves into alphabetical order again. Finish by reciting the alphabet.

## Extension/further reading

In PE, ask the children to work in pairs to create the letters of the alphabet with their bodies. Or ask them to work together to spell out each other's names with the shapes of their bodies. Use a digital camera to record the shapes made. Select one picture for each letter of the alphabet. Find objects that begin with the initial letters and display the images with the objects.

As well as the rest of *The Bad Day ABC*, you could read *Kipper's A to Z* by Mick Inkpen (Hodder) and *What's Inside?* by Satoshi Kitamura (Andersen Press).

**R W2:** knowledge of grapheme/phoneme correspondences through:
● hearing and identifying initial sounds in words
● reading letters that represent the sounds *a-z*

**R W3:** alphabetic and phonic knowledge through:
● sounding and naming each letter of the alphabet
● understanding alphabetical order through alphabet books, rhymes and songs

*highly alliterative; each animal's name begins with the next letter of the alphabet*

*alphabetical order*

*patterned text: 'A' or 'An' [creature] [past-tense verb]…*

*each line conveys an unusual, vivid image*

*speech verb; indicates how word was uttered*

*simple rhyme pattern*

*question*

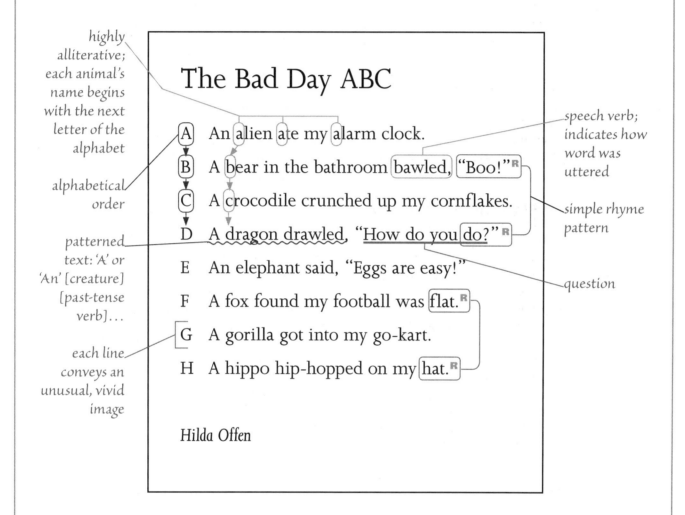

# The Bad Day ABC

A   An alien ate my alarm clock.

B   A bear in the bathroom bawled, "Boo!" ᴿ

C   A crocodile crunched up my cornflakes.

D   A dragon drawled, "How do you do?" ᴿ

E   An elephant said, "Eggs are easy!"

F   A fox found my football was flat. ᴿ

G   A gorilla got into my go-kart.

H   A hippo hip-hopped on my hat. ᴿ

Hilda Offen

**R W4:** to link sound and spelling patterns by: identifying alliteration in known and new and invented words

**R S3:** that words are ordered left to right and need to be read that way to make sense

**R S4:** to use a capital letter for the start of own name

**R T10:** to re-read and recite stories with predictable and repeated patterns and experiment with similar rhyming patterns

# A Week at Gran's by John Foster

## Background

The days of the week provide the structure for this narrative poem. It is a mini-story, with a series of episodic events, which has a satisfying conclusion as the children wave goodbye and look forward to their next visit. The poem is very simply organised, with straightforward language and few adjectives or adverbs, as is appropriate to the child's point of view, and an alternate-line rhyme scheme.

You could link this poem to 'Wolf's diary' (page 48).

## Shared reading and discussing the text

● Recap on the children's knowledge of the number of days in a week. Sequence them together, starting from *Monday*, and list them on the board. Draw attention to *day* as a word within a word, and that they all start with a capital letter. Display the list in the classroom for the children to refer to when writing and for familiarisation with the words.

● Read the poem a couple of times. Talk about the content of the poem and relate it to the children's experiences of holidays with grandparents or other family members. Ask them questions to enhance their appreciation of the poem, for example what indoor games might they have played on Tuesday? What kind of games and other entertainments are there at fairs? What kind of food might there be at a barbecue?

● Do they think the children in the poem enjoyed staying with Gran? Why? Ask which day they think was the most enjoyable for the children in the poem and why. Talk about how the last line would be read and practise reading it for the best effect.

● Show the children where the rhymes are, then re-read the poem, pausing to allow the children to predict the rhyming words.

## Activities

● Write a class sequence poem about different things the children have done when they have been on holiday. Use the form of 'A Week at Gran's', but your poem doesn't have to rhyme. List the days of the week and write one activity for each day. Display the poem where the children can read it.

● Go on an initial phoneme hunt, working with a small group at first. Ask the children if they can remember what happened on Friday in the poem. Re-read the lines, emphasising the initial letter *p*. Ask the children if they can hear anything special about certain words. If possible, show them a picture of one of the items from the poem (picnic, pool and park) emphasising the *p* as you say the word. Ask pairs of children to find objects in the classroom that start with the same letter. In a plenary session, ask the children what they have found. Confirm that the objects begin with *p*.

● Focus on the last four lines, but mask the word *Dad*. Read the lines together and ask the children to predict or recall the masked word. Reveal the word, letter by letter, encouraging the children to check their predictions as you go.

● Make a class noticeboard with a folder or box containing cards of changeable days of the week. List the activities for the day, for example *Today is Monday. Today's activities are singing and painting…* Talk about the noticeboard. Update it every day. Encourage the children to find the correct day to put up, and draw attention to the structure of the words to aid recognition.

## Extension/further reading

Read *From Snowflakes to Sandcastles* by Annie Owen (Frances Lincoln) to look at the months of the year. Cut out pictures from old calendars and talk with the children about what can be seen in the pictures. Using those that most obviously show the seasonal changes, play a sequencing game.

The children may also enjoy *Tweenies Days of the Week* (BBC), *My Days of the Week* by Siobhan Dodds (Franklin Watts) and the traditional rhyme 'Solomon Grundy'.

R W2: knowledge of grapheme/phoneme correspondences through:
● hearing and identifying initial sounds in words
● reading letters that represent the sounds *a-z*

R W4: to link sound and spelling patterns by: identifying alliteration in known words

R W5: to read on sight a range of familiar words

*list, diary format*

*1st person narrative*

*repeated high-frequency word*

*days of the week; topic words*

*capital letters for days*

*each day associated with new pleasure or activity*

*happy conclusion*

*words within words: 'sea', 'side'; 'in'*

*ABCB rhyme scheme*

*direct speech*

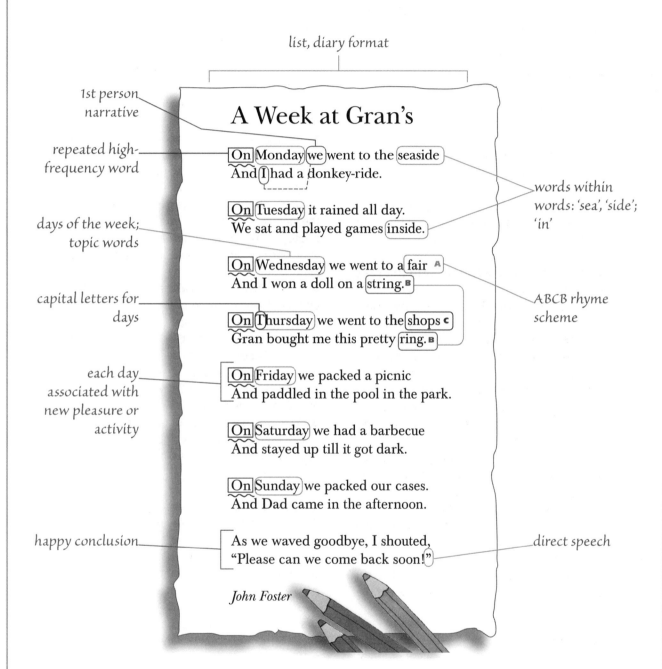

# A Week at Gran's

On Monday we went to the seaside
And I had a donkey-ride.

On Tuesday it rained all day.
We sat and played games inside.

On Wednesday we went to a fair ᴬ
And I won a doll on a string. ᴮ

On Thursday we went to the shops ᶜ
Gran bought me this pretty ring. ᴮ

On Friday we packed a picnic
And paddled in the pool in the park.

On Saturday we had a barbecue
And stayed up till it got dark.

On Sunday we packed our cases.
And Dad came in the afternoon.

As we waved goodbye, I shouted,
"Please can we come back soon!"

*John Foster*

R W6: to read on sight the 45 high-frequency words to be taught by the end of YR from Appendix List 1

R W9: to recognise the critical features of words, e.g. shape, length, and common spelling patterns

R T6: to re-read frequently a variety of familiar texts, e.g. poems

# Monsters

### by Linda Hammond

## Background

This poem is a modern version of a traditional number rhyme. It can be explored in a similar way to 'Five Ducks Five' (page 46). The text is very easy for children to follow and remember, with a highly predictable structure, repetition, regular rhyme scheme and strong rhythm. It also makes use of fun central characters and unusual events. It is a very useful text for allowing children to practise their subtraction skills.

## Shared reading and discussing the text

● Tell the children that they are going to learn a new counting rhyme. Read the text and show them that they can hold up five fingers at the start and take one away at the end of each verse. Ask the children if they know any other rhymes like this one. Remind them of 'Five Ducks Five', if they need prompting.

● 'Monsters' has a strong, recognisable rhythm. Encourage the children to accompany a re-reading of the rhyme with clapping.

● Read the rhyme again, pausing to encourage the children to supply the rhyming words and numbers. Give them time to enjoy the images and adventures created in the poem.

● Play an odd-one-out rhyme game. Pick one of the rhyming pairs, for example *sun/one*. Give the children a list of words (such as *sun, one done, fun, cat, bun*) and ask them to tell you which word doesn't belong to the rhyme family.

## Activities

● In shared or guided writing, extend the story by writing verses for ten monsters down to six. The repetitive structure provides a supportive framework, as only two lines in each verse need significant changes. Rhyming words for the numbers are needed (six: *sticks, tricks, bricks*; seven: *heaven*; eight: *gate, late, wait, mate*; nine: *fine, line, mine*) as well as places for the monsters to be and 'accidents' to happen to them. You could change the colour of the monsters too. Collect ideas, then write the verses together. Read the whole rhyme from ten to one.

● Make a counting book together. Collect a group of ten similar objects, for example ten teddy bears. Use a digital camera to take a photograph of them. Take one away and photograph the group again. Continue until all the teddies have been removed. Print the photographs and use them as illustrations for your number story entitled, for example, *Ten Tired Teddies*.

● Give a small group of children a tape recorder and ask them to recite and record the poem onto tape. Make the tape available with an enlarged copy of the text for other children to listen to. Tapes of similar recordings could be exchanged with another class. Alternatively, a collection of counting rhymes might be recorded for the nursery.

● Make number pictures using buttons, pasta, sweet wrappers and so on. Ask the children to help you label the pictures with the words *one, two, three* and so on.

## Extension/further reading

As a numeracy activity, play musical chairs for practice in taking one away. Limit the game to ten children and use ten chairs in a row. You could tell the children to pretend they are the purple monsters in the poem as they play. Place the chairs that are taken away in a new row. Draw the children's attention to how many chairs remain and how many chairs are in the new row.

Stella Blackstone's *My Granny Went to Market* (Barefoot Books) is a lovely, multicultural shopping trip; Quentin Blake's *Cockatoos* (Red Fox) continues the ten-animals counting theme. You could also read Penny Dale's *Ten Out of Bed* (Walker Books), and use the *Oxford Rhyming Dictionary* to help the children find rhymes for their own poems.

**R W1:** to understand and be able to thyme through:
- recognising, exploring and working with rhyming patterns
- extending these patterns by analogy, generating new and invented words in speech and spelling

**R W5:** to read on sight a range of familiar words

*cardinal numbers; countdown – one taken away with each verse*

*ABCB rhyme scheme*

*use of repeated opening*

*bizarre adventures*

*'-un' rhyme family:*
sun
fun
bun
run
one
none
done

# Monsters

Five purple monsters A
went out to explore. B
One fell down a hole, C
so that left four. B

Four purple monsters
went down to the sea.
One swam far away,
so that left three.

Three purple monsters
went out to the zoo.
One joined the lions,
so that left two.

Two purple monsters
went out in the sun. R
One got far too hot,
so that left one. R

One purple monster
went out to have fun. R
Lost his way going home,
so that left none. R

*Linda Hammond*

**R T6:** to re-read frequently a variety of familiar texts, e.g. big books, story books, taped stories with texts, poems, own and other children's writing

**R T10:** to re-read and recite stories and rhymes with predictable and repeated patterns and experiment with similar rhyming patterns

# Cats

by Eleanor Farjeon

## Background

This is a classic poem, with some unusual language (such as *frock*), potentially difficult long 'sentences' and lots of ideas, but it is nonetheless very accessible to young children and appealing in its subject matter. Re-reading should prove very fruitful. The poem has visual impact (a long, thin list of short phrases) as well as a regular rhyme scheme.

The poem could link with 'Let's Look at Animals' (page 68) and with work on developing the children's knowledge and understanding of the world.

## Shared reading and discussing the text

● Display photographs, paintings and figurines/ sculptures of different domestic cats.

● Talk to the children about their experience of cats. Does anyone have a pet cat? What do they look like? What sorts of things do cats like doing?

● Read the poem expressively. Does anyone recognise their cat from the poem? Talk about the huge variety and often unlikely or seemingly unsuitable places cats choose to sleep. Which would be the most comfortable? Introduce the term *cat nap* from cats' ability to sleep for short periods anywhere and often.

● Check the children's vocabulary; they may not recognise *frocks* as 'dresses', nor know *window-ledge*.

● Notice how the poem is structured. The first two lines introduce the topic, then the poem gives detail, and the final two lines repeat the opening, as a summary.

● Re-read the poem to the children, pausing to encourage them to predict the rhyming words and the final *Anywhere*.

## Activities

● As a whole class or large group, think about different words that describe the way cats move (*creeping, pouncing, stretching, scratching* and so on). Use this list to develop a short movement list-poem about cats.

● Make a story box to accompany the poem.

Place dolls' house furniture and a model cat in a box (about shoebox size). Encourage the children to play with the items to recreate the poem. Through discussion about their play, reinforce the children's knowledge of prepositions.

● Focus on the sound and spelling patterns of the CVC word *cat*. Say the sentence *I pat the cat* and ask the children if they notice anything about the words *pat* and *cat*. Encourage them to recognise the rhyme and the length of the words. Write the words *cat* and *pat*, drawing attention to the individual phonemes as you write them. Ask the children how many letter sounds they can hear in the word, then ask them to suggest more words that rhyme with *cat* and *pat*. Generate a list of real and, if appropriate, invented words. Select some of the words and use them to construct a sentence, reinforcing concepts of print (the order of letters and words and so on) as you write.

● Look at the high-frequency words *in* and *on* in the poem. Write out cloze sentences such as *My cat likes to sleep ___ boxes. My cat likes to sleep ___ the cupboard. My cat likes to sleep ___ a chair. My cat likes to sleep ___ an empty shoe. My cat likes to sleep ___ my lap.* Have a number of cards with the words *in* and *on* written on them. Read each sentence and ask the children to select the correct card to include in it. Accept all answers that make sense.

## Extension/further reading

Talk about looking after pets. Consider the pleasures and responsibilities of having a pet.

Read *Where's Spot?* by Eric Hill (Heinemann) to consolidate understanding of prepositions. Read a selection of poems that focus on different aspects of cats. Try *Cat in the Dark* edited by Fiona Waters (Frances Lincoln) and *My First Book of Animal Poems* edited by John Foster (OUP). For rhymes, look at *Pat the Cat* by Colin and Jacqui Hawkins (Dorling Kindersley) and *Drat That Fat Cat!* by Pat Thompson and Ailie Busby (Scholastic).

**50 Shared texts ● Year R**

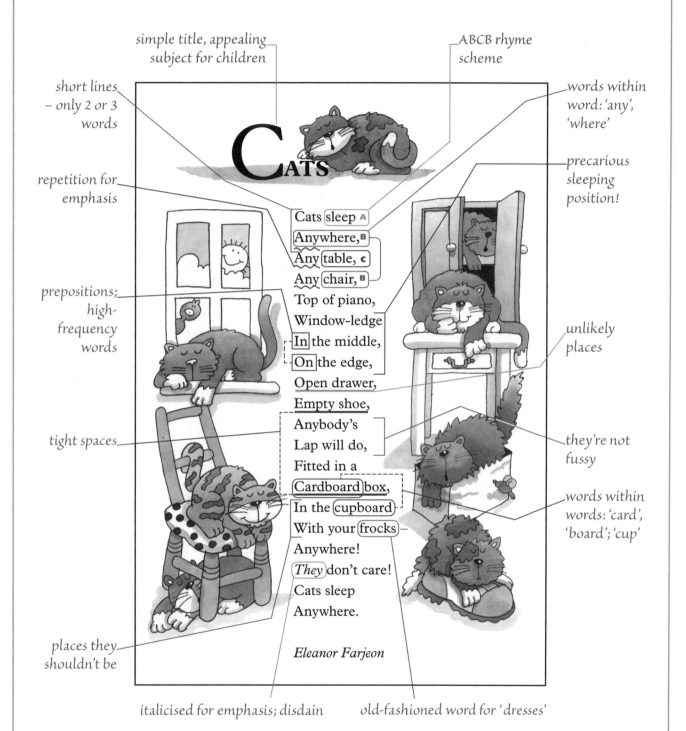

**R W4:** to link sound and spelling patterns by: using knowledge of rhyme to identify families of rhyming CVC words

**R W6:** to read on sight the 45 high-frequency words to be taught by the end of YR from Appendix List 1

**R W10:** new words from their reading and shared experiences

**R S3:** that words are ordered left to right and need to be read that way to make sense

simple title, appealing subject for children

ABCB rhyme scheme

short lines – only 2 or 3 words

words within word: 'any', 'where'

repetition for emphasis

precarious sleeping position!

prepositions; high-frequency words

unlikely places

tight spaces

they're not fussy

words within words: 'card', 'board'; 'cup'

places they shouldn't be

italicised for emphasis; disdain

old-fashioned word for 'dresses'

### CATS

Cats sleep A
Anywhere, B
Any table, C
Any chair, B
Top of piano,
Window-ledge
In the middle,
On the edge,
Open drawer,
Empty shoe,
Anybody's
Lap will do,
Fitted in a
Cardboard box,
In the cupboard
With your frocks
Anywhere!
*They* don't care!
Cats sleep
Anywhere.

*Eleanor Farjeon*

**R T7:** to use knowledge of familiar texts to re-enact or retell to others, recounting the main points in correct sequence

**R T11:** through shared writing:
● to understand how writing is formed directionally, a word at a time
● to understand how letters are formed and used to spell words

# What's in the Box?
by Trevor Millum

### Background

'What's in the Box?' is a poem that relates directly to most children's experiences and imaginations. It provides a question and answer structure, using a list format, that can be used as a model in shared writing. The poem uses two voices: a child asking; a parent, probably, answering; and the last verse could be both. The bouncy rhythm and rhyme scheme of rhyming couplets makes the poem very easy to follow and encourages prediction.

### Shared reading and discussing the text

● Show the children the title 'What's in the Box?'. Explain that the poem is about a toy box. What sorts of things do the children think might be found in the toy box?

● Read the text. Did the box contain the toys that the children imagined? Compare the contents of the toy box in the poem with the children's toy boxes.

● Ask the children why they think the teddy has only one eye. (Perhaps it is a well-loved, old toy, or it hasn't been looked after properly.)

● Re-read the last two lines of the first verse, drawing attention to the initial phoneme *b*. Then repeat the words *box*, *big* and *brass* and ask the children if they notice anything about them. Explain, if necessary, that they all start with the same sound, *b*. Ask if anyone in the class has a name beginning with *B*. Look around the room and encourage the children to identify objects that begin with the letter *b*.

● Re-read the poem, pausing to let the children predict the rhyming words.

### Activities

● List the items in the box and encourage the children in groups to recall the detail about each object: one-eyed ted, red ball, plastic boat and so on.

● Help the children to make a collage of the toys in the box, using pictures cut out of magazines and catalogues.

● Decorate a large cardboard box and gather a collection of objects including some that rhyme with *box* (fox, socks, clocks, locks, building blocks, rocks and so on). Tell the children that only objects that rhyme with *box* live in this box. Ask the children to decide which items can be put into the box. Display the game so that the children can play with it later.

● Ask the children to bring a special toy from home and to talk about why the toy is special. Take photographs of individual children with their toys and caption the pictures with phrases similar to those in 'What's in the box?'. Make a class book called *In Our Toy Box*.

● Assemble a collection of percussion instruments and ask the children to work in groups to match instruments to the toys, movements or sounds in the poem. Ask them, for example, which instrument makes a sound like a wind-up car, a clock that ticks or a plane that flies. Re-read the poem with the selected percussion sounds.

● Make a magnetic fishing game. Make a collection of picture cards, some showing objects that begin with the letter *b*. Attach paperclips to the cards. Make fishing rods from short pieces of dowelling and string with a small magnet tied on the end. Let the children fish in teams of two. Explain that the object of the game is to collect as many cards as they can which show objects that begin with *b*.

### Extension/further reading

Base a PE lesson on the toys. Collect some of the toys mentioned in the poem and consider their different movements: a ball can bounce or roll, a boat floats (or sinks). Imagine how the doll's arms, legs and head move. Take each toy in turn and ask the children to move as that toy. Encourage practice of movements using variations of level, pace and direction.

Read *Fox in Socks* by Dr Seuss (Picture Lions) to reinforce awareness of the *-ox* rhyme family. Other toy-related poems and stories include *All Aboard The Toy Train* collected by Tony Bradman (Hodder Wayland), Jane Hissey's *Old Bear Collection* (Hutchinson) and *Kipper's Toybox* by Mick Inkpen (Hodder Children's Books).

**R W1:** to understand and be able to rhyme through: recognising, exploring and working with rhyming patterns

**R W2:** knowledge of grapheme/phoneme correspondences through:
● hearing and identifying initial sounds in words
● reading letters that represent the sounds: *a-z*

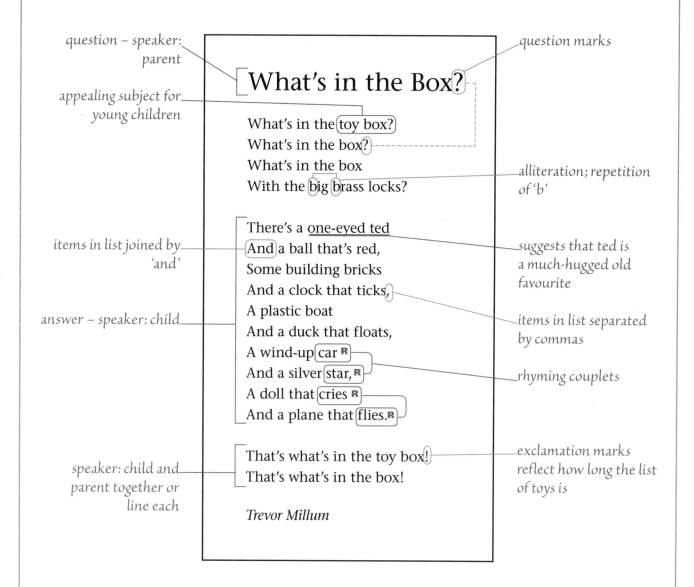

question – speaker: parent

appealing subject for young children

question marks

# What's in the Box?

What's in the toy box?
What's in the box?
What's in the box
With the big brass locks?

alliteration; repetition of 'b'

items in list joined by 'and'

There's a one-eyed ted
And a ball that's red,
Some building bricks
And a clock that ticks,
A plastic boat
And a duck that floats,
A wind-up car ℝ
And a silver star, ℝ
A doll that cries ℝ
And a plane that flies.ℝ

suggests that ted is a much-hugged old favourite

items in list separated by commas

answer – speaker: child

rhyming couplets

That's what's in the toy box!
That's what's in the box!

*Trevor Millum*

speaker: child and parent together or line each

exclamation marks reflect how long the list of toys is

**R W4:** to link sound and spelling patterns by: identifying alliteration in known and new words

**R T12:** through guided and independent writing: to write labels or captions for pictures and drawings

**R T15:** to use writing to communicate in a variety of ways, incorporating it into play and everyday classroom life, e.g. recounting their own experiences, labels

# The Apple and the Worm by Robert Heidbreder

## Background

This short, funny verse is easy to learn and is ideal for children to read aloud. The humour is derived from the situation, and from the rhyme and the enjoyment of the vocabulary used to describe the imagined sensation of swallowing a worm. The last lines of the poem take on a different format from the main body of the poem and make reference to the traditional rhyme 'There Was an Old Lady Who Swallowed a Fly'.

## Shared reading and discussing the text

● Tell the children the popular joke:

What's worse than finding a worm in an apple?
*Finding half a worm.*

Ask whether the joke is funny. Why (or why not)? Explain that you are going to read a poem about someone who swallows a worm when eating an apple.

● Read the text and discuss what the children like about it.

● What words are used to describe what the worm feels like when it has been swallowed? (For example, *squiggle, wiggle, slippery, slimy.*) What words might be used to describe a spider if it had been swallowed? (For example, *wriggly, tickly.*)

● Draw attention to the capitalised word *PLOP.* How should that word be read? If you can, show the children how a plopping sound can be made by pulling your finger along the inside of your cheek. Re-read the verse, adding the plopping sounds at the appropriate place and relishing the words that describe the worm's movement.

● Re-read the last verse and ask the children why swallowing a bird would get rid of the worm. Then consider what might get rid of the bird and so on. Follow this up by reading the traditional rhyme 'There Was an Old Lady Who Swallowed a Fly'.

## Activities

● Working with a small group, have a joke-telling session. Where do the children hear jokes? (In the playground, at home, on television, in books.) Encourage the children to share jokes, developing their confidence for speaking in small group situations.

● Create a large class zigzag story book in which a worm is swallowed in an apple, a bird is swallowed to catch the worm and so on. Caption the drawings with sentences, such as *I swallowed the bird to catch the worm.*

● Ask the children to make a large picture of the worm, perhaps peeking out of the apple. Add the words from the poem that describe the worm.

● Work with a small group to read the poem onto tape, allocating different sections of the text as appropriate. Encourage expressive reading of words that describe the worm's movements and *PLOP.* Include a pause after the ellipsis. Make the recording of the poem available with an enlarged version of the text.

● Draw attention to the alliterative qualities of the words *squiggle, squirm, slippery, slimy* and *scummy.* Ask the children if they can hear anything special about the sounds of these words. Can they think of any words to add to the list? (*Squishy, squashy, slithery* and so on.)

## Extension/further reading

Play a game called 'The hungry worm'. Explain that the worm is hungry but he can only eat fruit or vegetables. Ask the children to name, in turn, a fruit or vegetable that the worm could eat. Draw a group picture showing all the things that the worm can eat and caption it with *Our hungry worm can eat...*

Examine different kinds of apple. Cut up apples to look at seed patterns. Look at the growth of the apple through the seasons.

Read more poems from Jill Bennett's anthology *A Cup of Starshine* (Walker Books), *The Very Hungry Caterpillar* by Eric Carle (Puffin), and *The Apple* by Rod Hunt (OUP).

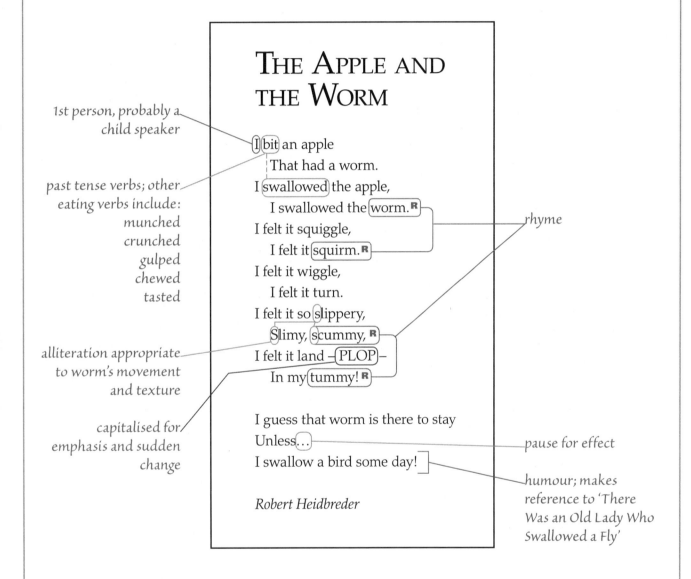

**R: W5:** to read on sight a range of familiar words

**R: T7:** to use knowledge of familiar texts to re-enact or retell to others, recounting the main points in correct sequence

**R: W10:** new words from their reading and shared experiences

1st person, probably a child speaker

past tense verbs; other eating verbs include:
munched
crunched
gulped
chewed
tasted

alliteration appropriate to worm's movement and texture

capitalised for emphasis and sudden change

## THE APPLE AND THE WORM

I bit an apple
That had a worm.
I swallowed the apple,
I swallowed the worm. **R**
I felt it squiggle,
I felt it squirm. **R**
I felt it wiggle,
I felt it turn.
I felt it so slippery,
Slimy, scummy, **R**
I felt it land – PLOP –
In my tummy! **R**

I guess that worm is there to stay
Unless...
I swallow a bird some day!

*Robert Heidbreder*

rhyme

pause for effect

humour; makes reference to 'There Was an Old Lady Who Swallowed a Fly'

**R: T12** through guided and independent writing: to experiment with writing and recognise how their own version matches and differs from conventional version

**R: T14** to use experience of poems as a basis for independent writing, e.g. retelling, substitution, extension, and through shared composition with adults

# Here is the Seed by John Foster

## Background

This poem is one of a group of texts focusing on plant growth (see 'Why do sunflowers face the sun?', page 70 and 'Children's Collection', page 72). The poem uses elements of traditional action rhymes (such as *Here is the church…*) and can be read with accompanying actions that show the growth from a tiny seed into a fully grown plant. The patterned language and simple ABCB rhyme scheme encourages prediction and recall.

## Shared reading and discussing the text

● Gather some sunflower seeds, soil, a plant pot and small watering can. Show the children the seeds and ask if they know what they are. Ask them if they know what makes seeds grow into flowers like the ones on the packet illustration. (Plants usually need sun, water and soil.) If you have any sunflowers in school, let the children take a look at them. Tell them that they are going to learn a rhyme about a tiny seed that grows into a flower.

● Read the poem aloud to the children. Ask them if they spotted the different things that help the seed to grow. (Being underneath the ground – soil; the sun; the shower.)

● Practise the accompanying actions:

*Here is the seed* (curl in a ball on the floor)
*Here is the shoot* (start to uncurl)
*Growing tall* (slowly standing)
*Here is the sun* (make a large circle with pointing finger)
*Here is the shower* (make delicate raindrop movements with fingers)
*Here are the petals / Here is the flower* (pretend to be a fully grown flower).

● Ask the children if they can hear anything special about the pair of words *small* and *tall*, and praise recognition of the rhyme. Read the poem again and ask the children to raise their hands or a special card each time they hear a rhyme. Stop when they do so and ask them to repeat the rhyming words.

## Activities

● In shared or guided writing, write a set of instructions to explain accompanying actions. Use a diagram to show each of the actions. (You might want to allocate certain sections to different groups.) Ask the children to suggest phrases or short sentences that can be used to explain how to do the actions. Display the captioned actions with a copy of the poem.

● Use the repeated sentence starter *Here is the…* to encourage the children to write their own sentences about, for example, one of their toys, an animal, a different plant, a car.

● Ask the children what words are used instead of *little* in the poem. (*Tiny* and *small*.) What word means the opposite of *small*? (*Big*.) Do the children know any other words that mean the same as *big*? Use the illustration on the packet of flower seeds, or from a book, to show how a small seed can grow into a large sunflower. Ask the children to draw captioned pictures of a small seed and a big flower.

● Use a range of percussion instruments to create a growing story. What sound can be used for the seed being planted in the ground? (Perhaps the triangle.) Encourage the children to think about ways in which the instruments can reproduce the idea of growth, for example by moving from low to high pitch. Experiment with different instruments. They can be played very quietly at the beginning of the piece and increase in volume as the plant grows. Narrate the poem with the children's accompaniments.

● Plan and create a garden centre in the imaginative play area. Include items such as plastic plant pots, seed packets, garden equipment, gardening books, a cash register. Write signs with the children, for example *Pay here*, price stickers and so on.

## Extension/further reading

Plant seeds and observe the plants' growth.

Books on this topic include *MyBees: A Seed in Need* (Hodder Wayland); *Plants: How Plants Grow* by Angela Royston (Heinemann) and *The Tiny Seed* by Eric Carle (Picture Puffins).

**R W1:** to understand and be able to rhyme through:
● recognising, exploring and working with rhyming patterns
● extending these patterns by analogy

**R T11:** through shared writing: to understand that writing can be used for a range of purposes

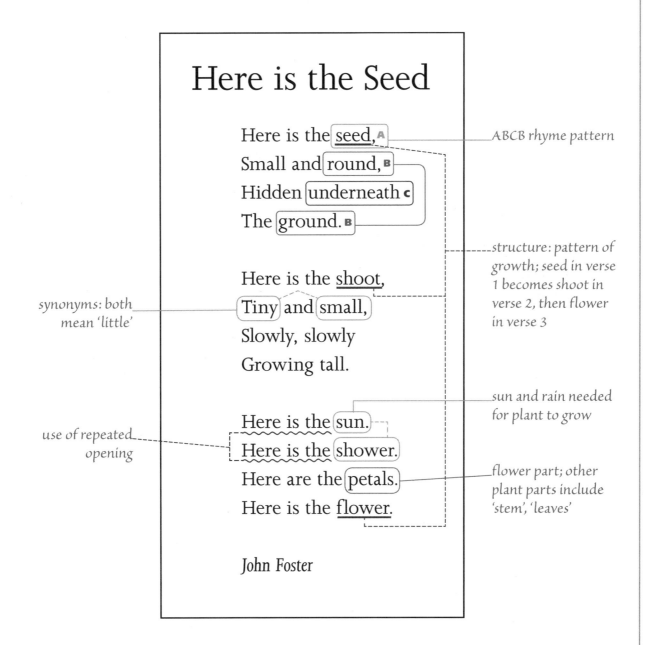

# Here is the Seed

Here is the seed, ▪A
Small and round, ▪B
Hidden underneath ▪c
The ground. ▪B

*ABCB rhyme pattern*

Here is the shoot,
Tiny and small,
Slowly, slowly
Growing tall.

*synonyms: both mean 'little'*

*structure: pattern of growth; seed in verse 1 becomes shoot in verse 2, then flower in verse 3*

Here is the sun.
Here is the shower.
Here are the petals.
Here is the flower.

*use of repeated opening*

*sun and rain needed for plant to grow*

*flower part; other plant parts include 'stem', 'leaves'*

John Foster

**R T12:** through guided and independent writing:
● to write labels or captions for pictures and drawings
● to write sentences to match pictures or sequences of pictures

**R T14:** to use experience of poems as a basis for independent writing, e.g. retelling, substitution, extension, and through shared composition with adults

# Let's Look at Animals by Nicola Tuxworth

### Background

This simple non-fiction text provides basic information about the characteristics of certain animals and asks direct questions to the reader to encourage involvement and discussion. Other characteristic features of information texts include the use of sub-headings, pictures and captions. Information is provided in photographs as well as in words.

### Shared reading and discussing the text

● Establish what the children already know about ducks. Write down a list of duck facts. Ask the children what questions about ducks they would like to find answers to and write these suggestions down too.

● Read the first section, drawing attention to the title and sub-heading. Ask the children whether they have learned anything new.

● Draw attention to the word *duckling*. Ask the children if they can find another word hiding inside *duckling*. Ask a volunteer to find the word *duck* and highlight it.

● Repeat the process with rabbits.

● Focus on animal movements. Re-read the first two sentences on each animal and ask the children which words describe how the animals move. (*Hop, walk, fly, swim.*) Encourage the children to think about words that describe different animal movements, such as those of snails, butterflies and frogs.

● Look at the photographs and consider what information they tell us about the animals. For example, they help us see the animals' shapes and markings. What other information do they provide?

### Activities

● In shared writing, use the text as a model for producing an information text about another animal, letting the children decide which one. Suggest they choose an animal they are interested in but do not yet know much about.

● Collect pictures of baby animals, then, working in small groups, help the children to make a book called *Animal Babies*. Re-read the sentence *A baby duck is called a duckling*. Look at each of the animal pictures and ask the children if they know the names given to them. Include some well-known examples (cat – kitten, dog – puppy, sheep – lamb) and some that might be less familiar to the children (elephant – calf, horse – foal, fox – cub). Make a list of these. Use the model sentence *A baby ___ is called a ___* for the children to use in writing about their pictures. Draw attention to the capital letter at the beginning of the sentence and the full stop at the end. Remind the children to think about how to fill the gaps in the sentence before they begin writing, discussing it within their group if necessary.

● Play a 'What am I?' game with a group, using a collection of animal pictures (young and adult). Choose one animal for the children to describe. Working around the circle, each child gives one sentence describing the animal. Encourage them to think of size, colour, movement, noise, habitat and so on. Combine the sentences to write an information text about the animal. A variation of the game is for children to think of an animal and describe it to the rest of the group, who then try to work out which animal is being described. Give praise for accuracy and observation of details. Set a challenge to describe a less familiar animal.

● Produce some cloze sentences based on the text for children to complete with appropriate verbs. For example, *A duck can ___ on land. A duck can ___ in ponds or rivers.*

### Extension/further reading

Ask the children to bring in photographs of pets. In circle time, encourage the children to talk about their pets. Make a class book with the pictures and accompanying captions.

Visit a farm that has ducks and rabbits.

Books on the topic include *Looking after my Pet Rabbit* (Lorenz Books), *Make Way for Ducklings* by Robert McCloskey (Viking Press), *Duck* in Dorling Kindersley's *See How They Grow* series and *Pet Poems* compiled by Jennifer Curry (Scholastic).

*title*

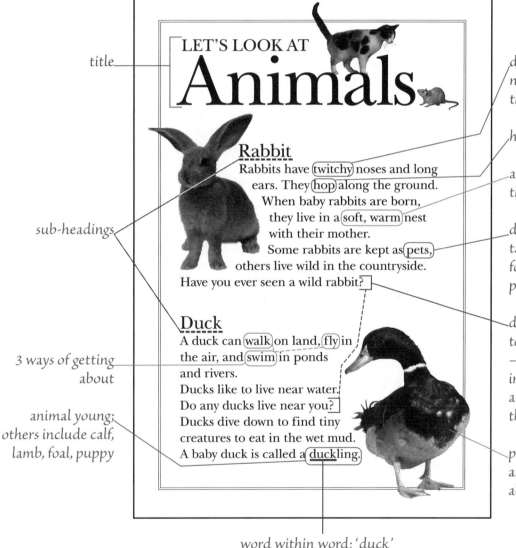

## LET'S LOOK AT
# Animals

### Rabbit
Rabbits have twitchy noses and long ears. They hop along the ground. When baby rabbits are born, they live in a soft, warm nest with their mother.
Some rabbits are kept as pets, others live wild in the countryside. Have you ever seen a wild rabbit?

### Duck
A duck can walk on land, fly in the air, and swim in ponds and rivers.
Ducks like to live near water.
Do any ducks live near you?
Ducks dive down to find tiny creatures to eat in the wet mud.
A baby duck is called a duckling.

*describes how the noses appear, how they move*

*how rabbits move*

*adjectives describe the nest*

*domesticated, tame animals kept for company and pleasure*

*direct questions to the reader – encourages involvement and interactive thinking*

*photographs of the animals written about*

*sub-headings*

*3 ways of getting about*

*animal young; others include calf, lamb, foal, puppy*

*word within word: 'duck'*

# Why do sunflowers face the sun?

## Background

This extract uses a series of questions as sub-headings and gives the answers as the main text. It provides a good introductory model for children's information texts, as it explicitly demonstrates that books can be used for finding answers to questions that readers have about the world. It links to other texts on growth – 'Here is the Seed' (page 66), 'Let's Look at Animals' (page 68) and 'Children's Collection' (page 72).

## Shared reading and discussing the text

● Prior to reading, gather a range of picture resources showing sunflowers and cactuses.

● Ask the children if they have ever wondered why certain things are the way they are, for example why the sky is blue. Briefly share their 'I wonder why' questions and encourage any answers other children may be able to suggest. Explain that you are going to read a text called 'Why do sunflowers face the sun?'. Ask whether anyone knows the answer. Note sensible answers, then say that you are going to read the text so they can see if they were right.

● Read the first question together, showing the direction of the text from left to right. Explain why the question mark has been used.

● Read the answer and check the children's understanding of vocabulary such as *landing pads* and *energy-giving light.*

● Read the second question and its answer. Briefly talk about whether the children water plants in their homes and gardens, and any you have in the classroom. Is it possible to give a plant too much water? Highlight the word *rainwater.* Ask if anyone can find smaller words hiding in rainwater (*rain* and *water*). Can a different word be found? (Also *in* and *ate.*)

● Ask whether any of the children own or have seen a cactus. Ask them to describe what it was like in terms of shape, colour and texture. Show pictures of different cactuses, then read the third question and answer. Help the children to understand the word *precious.* Why is rainwater described as precious in this instance?

● Consolidate understanding of -*est* superlative words (see also 'The Three Billy Goats Gruff', page 76). Re-read the first sentence about cactuses, pausing to point out the superlatives: *Cactuses are the roughest* (most rough), *toughest* (most tough) *plants in the desert.*

● Ask a series of questions using superlatives, for example *Which is the prickliest plant? Which is the tallest plant?* Children should be able to answer within the scope of their experience.

## Activities

● In a small group, identify some of the children's 'I wonder why' questions. They may need support in framing questions to which you or they will be able to locate answers. The range of questions can be limited by providing a focus, such as questions about birds. Choose one question to investigate. Use the Internet and a range of sources to help the children find an answer. Model writing the question as one short sentence and the answer as a few sentences, if appropriate. Reinforce knowledge about sentences, for example does it make sense, does it have a full-stop and capital letter, does the question have a question mark? Ask the children to find or draw pictures to go with their text.

● Show the children that some plants bought in garden centres have care labels. Using these and the information given in the extract, help the children to write instructions for caring for pot plants (see also 'Children's Collection', page 72). Ask the children what a plant needs to grow and keep healthy. These care instructions can be displayed in the 'garden centre' with other posters and signs.

## Extension/further reading

Arrange a visit from a keen amateur gardener, or a professional gardener, to talk to the children about gardening.

For further ideas, try *Garden Fun!* by Vicky Congdon (Williamson Publishing) and *Flower Garden* by Eve Bunting (Harcourt Brace).

**R S1:** to expect written text to make sense and to check for sense if it does not

**R T1:** through shared reading: to understand and use correctly terms about books and print: *book, cover, beginning, end, page, line, word, letter, title*

**R T3:** to re-read a text to provide context cues to help read unfamiliar words

words within words: 'sun', 'flower'; 'rain', 'water'

questions used as sub-headings; questions often start with 'Why'

where flying insects come down to stop

sunlight helps plant make its food

# WHY

## DO SUNFLOWERS FACE THE SUN?

**Why do sunflowers turn towards the sun?**
Sunflowers' beautiful, yellow heads and green leaves follow the sun across the sky, making warm landing pads for bees and catching lots of energy-giving light.

**Why do plants have to be watered?**
Next time it rains, think about the plants outside. They use rainwater to make food and to hold up their leaves. Indoor plants would die if we didn't give their thirsty roots a drink.

**Why do cactuses have prickles?**
Cactuses are the roughest, toughest plants in the desert. Their sharp prickles protect them from hungry animals and collect precious water from dewdrops.

direct address to reader

most rough

most tough

facts given in answers

dry area of land, often sandy

something of great value and, in this case, rarity

**R T11:** through shared writing:
● to understand that writing can be used for a range of purposes, e.g. to inform
● to understand how writing is formed directionally, a word at a time

**R T12:** through guided and independent writing: to write sentences to match pictures or sequences of pictures

# Children's Collection

### Background

This set of instructions taken from the back of a seed packet is a form of procedural text that may be familiar to very young children. It is best if the children have opportunities to plant cress seeds to make the experience meaningful.

Typical features include steps that must be followed in the correct order and imperative verbs (words that tell us to do something).

### Shared reading and discussing the text

● Create a stimulus display of distinctive seeds with photographs of the plants that grow from them, for example acorn, coconut, poppy, horse chestnut, sunflower.

● Prior to reading gather together some cress seeds, kitchen paper, a saucer, a plastic bag and tie. Ask the children whether they have ever grown anything from a seed. *What did you grow? Did the seeds come out of a packet? Where can you buy packets of seeds? Do seeds always come in a packet?*

● Show the text and explain that it is from a seed packet. Read it through, highlighting key features, such as the title and the imperative verbs (*put, sprinkle, seal, place* and so on). Help the children to notice that these words all tell the reader what to do. If growing cress, carry out each step as you re-read the instructions.

● Consider why instructions are printed on the seed packet. What would happen if clear instructions were not given? Explain that although the instructions are not numbered, they should be followed in order. With some of the remaining items, show what happens if the steps are carried out in the wrong order. For example, *the (empty) saucer is put in the bag; seed is sprinkled over (any) paper...*

● The last 'instruction' is a piece of advice: that cress is tasty in salads. Ask the children what other words they could use to say that they enjoy the taste of something. (Perhaps *delicious, yummy, scrumptious*).

● Draw attention to *packet contents*: a list of different seeds that the packet contains, the items separated by commas.

### Activities

● Help the children, in groups, to follow the instructions for growing cress and record what has been done in words or pictures.

● Provide the children with sheets of paper divided into four boxes. Give out a set of cards (text or pictures according to the children's reading ability) with four simplified stages of growing cress – planting, putting it in a dark cupboard, watching it grow, eating cress sandwiches. Ask the children to place the cards in the correct order, then draw each of the stages. Encourage more able children to caption their pictures.

● As a class, ask the children to imagine what their ideal garden would be like. Discuss the sorts of things that would be included. Create a drawing or collage of the garden from the children's suggestions.

● Re-read the instructions with a group. Ask the children how they can contact the suppliers if they wanted a catalogue showing all the different kinds of seed they could buy. Read the address. Write out the address and ask the children to help you compose a letter requesting a catalogue.

● Using an interactive whiteboard and graphics package, design a seed packet for sunflower seeds. Encourage the children to suggest colours, images, font style and font size. Key words can be programmed into the software to aid word recognition.

### Extension/further reading

Use a sound collage to create the different noises that might be heard in the garden the children have created. Create an accompanying movement and drama piece. Ask the children to use their bodies to represent different features of the garden (trees, water, prickly roses, birds, leaves rustling and so on).

Suggested non-fiction and activity books are *I Can Grow Things* by Sally Walton and Stephanie Donaldson and *Let's look at Flowers* (both Lorenz Books). Eric Carle's *The Tiny Seed* (Picture Puffins) puts explanation within a story.

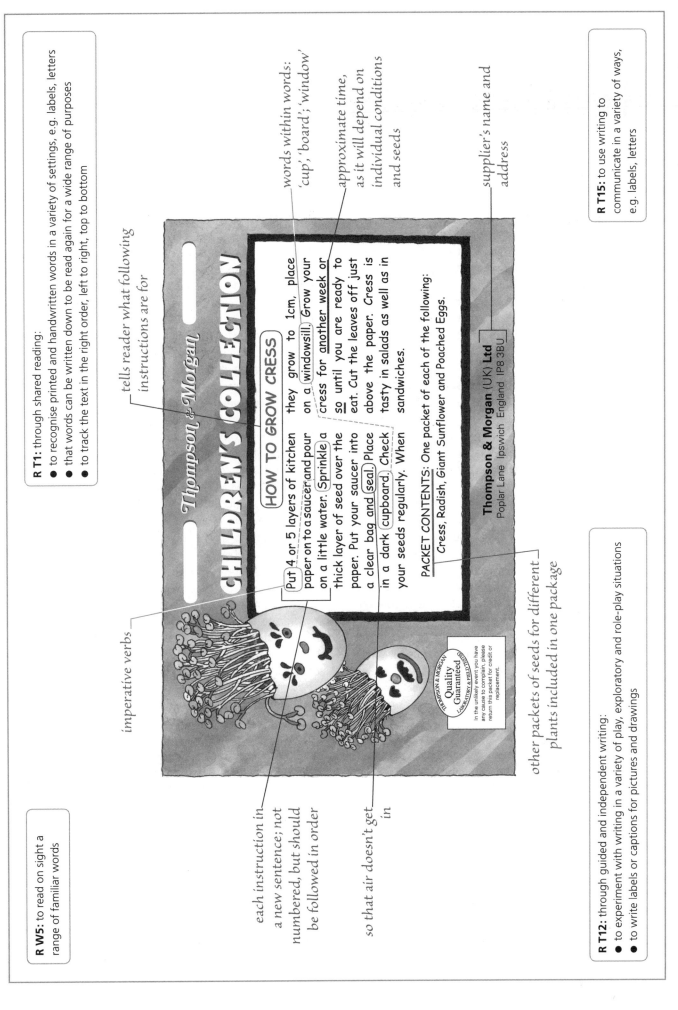

**R T1:** through shared reading:
- to recognise printed and handwritten words in a variety of settings, e.g. labels, letters
- that words can be written down to be read again for a wide range of purposes
- to track the text in the right order, left to right, top to bottom

tells reader what following instructions are for

words within words: 'cup'; 'board'; 'window'

approximate time, as it will depend on individual conditions and seeds

supplier's name and address

**R T15:** to use writing to communicate in a variety of ways, e.g. labels, letters

imperative verbs

**CHILDREN'S COLLECTION**

*Thompson & Morgan*

**HOW TO GROW CRESS**

Put 4 or 5 layers of kitchen paper onto a saucer and pour on a little water. Sprinkle a thick layer of seed over the paper. Put your saucer into a clear bag and seal. Place in a dark cupboard. Check your seeds regularly. When they grow to 1cm, place on a windowsill. Grow your cress for another week or so until you are ready to eat. Cut the leaves off just above the paper. Cress is tasty in salads as well as in sandwiches.

PACKET CONTENTS: One packet of each of the following: Cress, Radish, Giant Sunflower and Poached Eggs.

**Thompson & Morgan** (UK) **Ltd**
Poplar Lane Ipswich England IP8 3BU

THOMPSON & MORGAN
Quality
Guaranteed
LABORATORY & FIELD TESTED
In the unlikely event you have any cause to complain, please return this packet for credit or replacement.

**R W5:** to read on sight a range of familiar words

each instruction in a new sentence; not numbered, but should be followed in order

so that air doesn't get in

other packets of seeds for different plants included in one package

**R T12:** through guided and independent writing:
- to experiment with writing in a variety of play, exploratory and role-play situations
- to write labels or captions for pictures and drawings

# Weather map

## Background

Children will be familiar with weather map images from the television and possibly from the Internet. Maps like these use symbols to represent different types of weather. A key provides a definition of the symbols. Children can learn the conventional symbols, find different ones that are used and invent their own.

## Shared reading and discussing the text

● Ask the children if they have seen the weather forecast on television. At what time is the weather forecast normally shown? (At the end of the news.) What sorts of pictures are shown when the presenter is telling us about the weather? (For example, maps, satellite photographs, regional video footage.) You may want to make a recording of a simple weather forecast and view it with the children.

● Explain that a weather forecast predicts what the weather will be like tomorrow or later in the week. Consider some reasons that a weather forecast might be useful. Gather ideas from the children and extend their understanding with your suggestions, for example it helps us decide what clothes we should wear; whether it will be a good day for going to the seaside; helps fishermen prepare for stormy weather and farmers to harvest their crops before the rain comes.

● Look at the map together. Ask the children if they know what the area shown on the map is called. (United Kingdom.) Ask the children if they can point out the area of the country in which they live. Mark your home town/city/ village on the map.

● Ask the children if they can work out what type of weather is represented by each of the symbols.

● Introduce the concept of north, south, east and west by indicating different areas on the map. Ask the children if they have heard these words before. Ask what weather is forecast for the north of the country. Repeat for other areas.

## Activities

● In the imaginative play area, set up a laminated, blank version of the map with a collection of symbols that can be attached with Blu-Tack. Provide a pointer so that children can role-play presenting the weather forecast. You may want to have the video recording of a weather forecast available in the play area.

● Ask the children to create their own symbols for different types of weather. Share the symbols and see if the other children can recognise the weather they represent.

● Explain that each day you are going to record the weather by placing the correct symbol on the map. At the beginning of the day, ask the children to describe the weather. Attach a symbol to the weather map. Underneath, scribe *Today is _____* (for example, *windy*).

● Use the daily recording to complete a weather chart using the days of the week. Produce a two-column table with seven rows. In shared writing, write the days of the week in the left-hand column, drawing attention to the structure of the words and encouraging the children to recognise the word within a word, *day*. In the right-hand column, record the weather each day. Review the chart at the end of the week.

## Extension/further reading

The weather map can be used as a stimulus for musical interpretation. Choose from a range of percussion instruments to represent different types of weather. The children can take it in turns to read the weather and play appropriate instruments.

Extend the children's general observations of the weather by introducing some simple ways of observing and recording. For example, introduce the idea of measuring the wind by devising a simple windsock.

Read some traditional stories about the weather, such as *Tales of the Shimmering Sky* retold by Susan Milord (Williamson Publishing Company) and *The Weather Drum* by Rosalind Kerven (CUP).

**R W10:** new words from their reading and shared experiences

**R T1:** through shared reading:
● to recognise printed and handwritten words in a variety of settings, e.g. labels, signs
● that words can be written down to be read again for a wide range of purposes

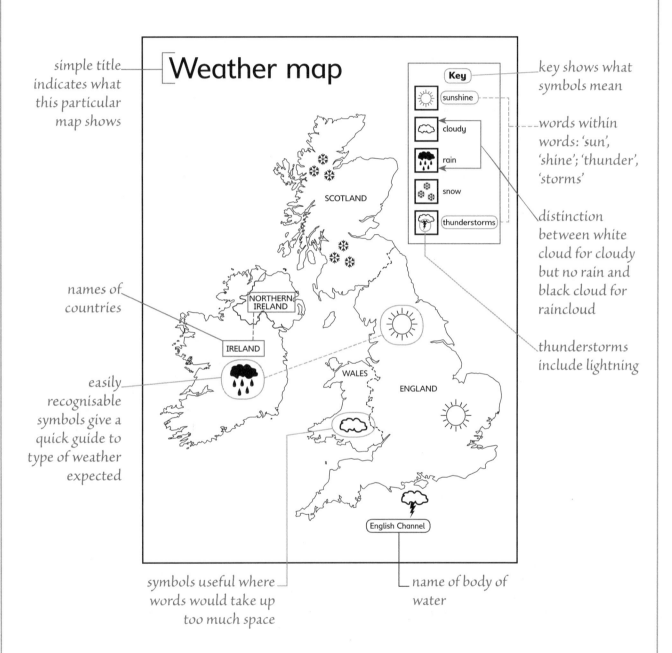

*simple title indicates what this particular map shows*

# Weather map

*key shows what symbols mean*

*words within words: 'sun', 'shine'; 'thunder', 'storms'*

*distinction between white cloud for cloudy but no rain and black cloud for raincloud*

*thunderstorms include lightning*

*names of countries*

*easily recognisable symbols give a quick guide to type of weather expected*

*symbols useful where words would take up too much space*

*name of body of water*

**R T11:** through shared writing: to understand how letters are formed and used to spell words

**R T15:** to use writing to communicate in a variety of ways, incorporating it into play and everyday classroom life

# The Three Billy Goats Gruff
retold by Nikki Gamble   *Extract 1*

## Background
'The Three Billy Goats Gruff' is a traditional folktale from Norway that the children may be familiar with already in some fashion. It features a refrain that they can quickly learn and join in with. It uses some typical folk/fairy tale devices and simplifications: three 'good' characters versus one 'evil' or at least scary one; the bad character shown to be foolish and easily tricked; some kind of moral or message.

## Shared reading and discussing the text
● Collect some pictures of goats from the Internet (for example from www.yahooligans.com) and other sources, such as books, resource magazines, farm park brochures and so on. Talk about the pictures. Draw attention to the horns and hooves. Talk about where goats tend to live, such as on farms and in the mountains. Ask the children to think about the noise that would be made by hooves on a wooden bridge.

● Read the extract, then ask the children what they think will happen next.

● In the story the troll is described as fierce. When he talks it says he *growled*. Why do they think the troll doesn't want the goats to cross his bridge? (Perhaps because it is *his* bridge; he wants to eat them; he is cross at being woken up by the sound of their hooves.)

● Explore different ways of reading the dialogue to highlight its use in characterisation. For example, read '*Who's that trip-trapping over my bridge?*' as if the words are spoken by an angry troll, a timid troll, a friendly troll. Draw attention to the capitalised speech '*I'M GOING TO EAT YOU UP!*', and ask the children why it is written like this. (To show it is said/shouted loudly and with feeling.)

● The story says that the goat *trip-trapped* and *clattered* over the bridge. Ask the children to describe what sort of noise *clattered* is.

## Activities
● Draw an outline picture of the troll and one of the billy goats and add large cut-out speech bubbles. Ask the children to recall the first words spoken by the troll. Write the words in his speech bubble. Draw attention to the structure of the words as you write them. Do the same for the billy goat. What does he say in reply to the troll? ('*It is only me.*')

● In speech bubbles, write some of the dialogue from the story, for example *Who's that trip trapping over my bridge?*, *If you let me pass...* Read them one at a time with the children and ask which character spoke those words. Attach the speech bubbles to the correct character outlines.

● Provide a range of art materials for the children to create images of the troll.

● Play a game for the initial phoneme *g*. Gather a collection of objects, some beginning with *g*. Seat the children in a circle with space for the troll's bridge. Write the title 'The Three Billy Goats Gruff' on a sheet of paper, speaking the words as you write. Ask the children if they can hear anything special about the beginning of the words *goat* and *gruff* and confirm that both words begin with the same phoneme, *g*. Explain that the troll who lives under the bridge has promised that he won't bully the billy goats again and will always let anyone holding an object that begins with the same phoneme as *goat* and *gruff* cross the bridge. Ask a more able child to play the part of the troll. The other children should take turns to pick up an object that begins with *g*. The troll will ask, *What have you brought me?* and if it is confirmed that the object begins with *g*, that player can 'cross the bridge'.

● Help the children make simple puppets of the troll and the billy goats, using paper plates and lollipop sticks. In small groups, encourage the children to use their puppets to retell the story.

## Extension/further reading
Other versions of the tale include those by Ted Dewan (Scholastic), Mary Finch (Barefoot Books). Related titles are *The Grumpy Goat* by Heather Amery (Usborne) and *The Toll-bridge Troll* by Patricia Rae Wolff (Harcourt Brace).

**R W2:** knowledge of grapheme/phoneme correspondences through: hearing and identifying initial sounds in words

**R S2:** to use awareness of the grammar of a sentence to predict words during shared reading and when re-reading familiar stories

**R T5:** to understand how story book language works and to use some formal elements when retelling stories, e.g. *Once there was…*

# The Three Billy Goats Gruff

*Extract 1*

*typical traditional story language*

*superlatives*

*problem becomes complicated*

*synonyms include: small tiny teeny*

*problem is solved for first goat*

Once, by the bank of a river, there lived three Billy Goats Gruff. They were very happy for they had all the grass they could eat. But one day the smallest Billy Goat Gruff said to his brothers, "Let's cross the river; the grass looks much greener and sweeter on the other side."

His brothers agreed that the grass did look greener and sweeter, and they decided to cross the little wooden bridge over the river, one at a time.

But a fierce troll lived under the bridge.

When the little goat clattered across the bridge, the fierce troll jumped up and growled in his scariest voice, "Who's that trip-trapping over my bridge?"

"It is only me," said the little billy goat.

"I'M GOING TO EAT YOU UP!"

"If you let me pass, my bigger brother will cross the bridge, and he is much larger and juicier than me," said the little goat.

"Very well," said the troll, and he let the little goat go over the bridge.

*pattern of 3 common in traditional tales*

*introduces characters and setting*

*introduces a problem*

*hard rattling sound*

*menacing animal sound; similar verbs are 'snarl', 'bellow' and 'roar'*

*comparatives*

**R T7:** to use knowledge of familiar texts to re-enact or retell to others, recounting the main points in correct sequence

**R T8:** to locate and read significant parts of the text, e.g. picture captions, names of key characters, rhymes and chants, e.g. *'I'm a troll…', 'You can't catch me I'm the Gingerbread Man…',* speech bubbles, italicised, enlarged words

# The Three Billy Goats Gruff

retold by Nikki Gamble  *Extract 2*

### Background

The second extract continues the story. In common with similar traditional tales, the troll is outwitted by the ingenuity of the goats. The ending is a happy one for the goats, who can eat the sweeter, greener grass in peace.

### Shared reading and discussing the text

● Ask the children to recall the first part of the story. Use questions and prompts to pick up important details.

● Read the extract, drawing attention to text features and concepts about print. For example, show that you start reading on the left-hand side of the page and read across; when you reach the end of the line, you return to the left on the line below. Notice the capital letters for names such as *Billy Goat Gruff,* and capitalisation at the beginning of speech.

● Recall the children's predictions about what would happen in this extract. Were they right? Ask the children if they liked the story. Why? Ask whether it reminds them of any other stories they are familiar with.

● The last billy goat is the *biggest.* Explain that this means there wasn't a bigger goat. Ask the children to think of other superlatives. For example, the most sad goat would be the *saddest,* the most happy goat would be the *happiest.* Remind them of the first little billy goat: *He is smaller than the other two, so he is the… smallest.*

### Activities

● Provide a set of story cards with illustrations of different parts of the story on each card. Encourage the children to use the cards for sequencing and retelling the story.

● Help the children to retell the story using percussion instruments to make the sounds of the billy goats' hooves. Choose a different instrument, such as different types of drum, for each of the billy goats, drawing attention to the size and the need to make the loudest noise for the biggest goat.

● Make a simplified big book version of the story with the class or group. Include key words or sentences from the two extracts in your book, for example *Who's that trip-trapping over my bridge?*

● Provide small groups of children with very large sheets of paper and encourage them to collaborate on drawing the story of the three Billy Goats Gruff. Group drawing is an exciting way of encouraging storytelling and language development.

● Ask the children to imagine what it would be like to be one of the characters in this story. Why is the troll so fierce and grumpy? Perhaps he has had a bad day. Perhaps he was trying to sleep under the bridge and the noise of the billy goats' hooves disturbed his rest. Ask different children to take on the role of the troll and answer questions from the rest of the class. The billy goats can also be hot-seated to show a different point of view.

● Shared writing can develop from the hot-seating. A letter might be written from the billy goats to the troll apologising for waking him up. Alternatively, the troll might write to apologise for frightening the younger billy goats.

● In shared writing, make a story plan based on the tale. List the characters; describe the setting; identify the problems; list the important events; write how the problem is overcome. Some children might then be able to use the story plan as a prompt for their own rewriting of the story.

### Extension/further reading

Devise a short play version of the story that can be produced and performed for another class or in assembly.

Read a selection of folk tales from a range of cultures, for example *Tales Alive!* by Susan Milord (Williamson) and other traditional stories, such as *Jack and the Beanstalk* by Nick Sharratt and Stephen Tucker (Macmillan Children's Books).

**R T5:** to understand how story book language works and to use some formal elements when retelling stories, e.g. *Once there was… She lived in a little…*

**R T7:** to use knowledge of familiar texts to re-enact or retell to others, recounting the main points in the correct sequence

# The Three Billy Goats Gruff

*Extract 2*

*size and order: small, medium, large; first, next, last*

Next came the middle Billy Goat Gruff. As he clattered across the bridge, the fierce troll jumped up and growled in his scariest voice, "Who's that trip-trapping over my bridge?"

*alliterative*

"It is only me," said the middle billy goat. "I'M GOING TO EAT YOU UP!"

*dialogue*

If you let me pass, my bigger brother will cross the bridge, and he is much larger and juicier than me," said the middle-sized goat.

"Well, alright," said the troll, who was getting very hungry indeed, and he let the middle-sized goat go over the bridge.

*story language*

Last of all came the oldest and biggest Billy Goat Gruff. As he clattered loudly onto the bridge, the fierce troll jumped up and growled in his scariest voice, "Who's that trip-trapping over my bridge?"

*capitals show speech is loud and sudden*

"ME!" roared the biggest billy goat. He charged across the bridge and butted the troll headlong into the river. The troll was swept away and nobody ever heard of him again.

*surprise image of scary, fierce billy goat*

*happy ending for goats*

But the Billy Goats Gruff lived for a long time and enjoyed the sweet, delicious grass on the other side of the river.

**R T8:** to locate and read significant parts of the text, e.g. italicised, enlarged words

**R T9:** to be aware of story structures, e.g. actions/reactions, consequences, and the ways that stories are built up and concluded

**R T13:** to think about and discuss what they intend to write, ahead of writing it

# Chicken Licken

Traditional

*Extract 1*

### Background

'Chicken Licken' is a traditional story with a very simple structure and repeating pattern. The repetition of dialogue allows the children to develop familiarity with the text, encourages them to join in with the reading and supports matching of text and speech.

### Shared reading and discussing the text

● Ask the children if they have heard the story of Chicken Licken. Can they remember what happens?

● Read the text aloud expressively. Discuss why Chicken Licken thinks the sky is falling.

● Ask the children what they notice about the names of the characters. (They all have rhyming names.) See if the children can generate rhymes for their own names. This may be difficult or sensitive for some children, so let them generate rhymes for your name or a familiar object.

● Re-read the extract, drawing attention to the story opening, *One day.* What other words are often used to start a story?

● Ask pairs of children to retell the story and predict what will happen.

● Share some of the children's predictions for the next part of the story, offering praise where clues from the text or knowledge of other stories has been used to inform the prediction.

### Activities

● Prepare a simple illustration of Chicken Licken, showing the acorn falling from the tree. Ask the children what they think Chicken Licken felt when he thought the sky was falling, for example surprised, worried, scared, frightened, shocked. List the suggested words. Tell the children you are going to write a sentence together that explains how Chicken Licken was feeling. Ask the children what you should write. Scribe the sentence, drawing attention to features such as the capital letter and full stop, thinking aloud and re-reading to check that what you have written makes sense.

● In groups, help the children to retell the story in a specified number of pictures, perhaps four.

Model writing a caption for one of the pictures and encourage the children to have a go at the rest independently.

● As a cloze activity, mask selected words in the extract that the children will be able to predict using context cues. As a guide, no more than one word in twenty should be masked. Read the text together. When you come to a masked word, ask the children to think of a meaningful word to replace the blank. Say, for example, *What do you think the next word will be?* Encourage them to think about the suitability of their suggestions: *Would that make sense? Would that sound right?* Reveal the word, accepting any of the children's suggestions that do make sense, and use this to reinforce knowledge about the structure of words (initial letter, final letter, that letters represent sounds).

● Present a range of percussion instruments and encourage the children to make a musical interpretation of the text. Ask them to consider which instrument could be played for the acorn dropping from the tree. Can a falling sound be made with any of the instruments? What sound could be played when the acorn lands on Chicken Licken's head? Should the sound be loud? Low or high? Short or long? Then choose an instrument to represent each animal. Re-read the story with accompaniment.

● The animals in the story all have rhyming names that use the *l* phoneme. Play a simple rhyming game in which the children select an object from a collection you have made and provide the rhyme for the object, for example *pen len, box lox.*

### Extension/further reading

Ask the children to select their favourite traditional stories and produce a display of 'Our favourite tales'.

Other versions of the story include those by Jonathan Allen (Corgi) and Michael Foreman (Red Fox) or you could listen to *The Puffin Book of Five-Minute Animal Stories* read by Imelda Staunton and Jim Carter.

**R S1:** to expect written text to make sense and to check for sense if it does not

**R S2:** to use awareness of the grammar of a sentence to predict words during shared reading and when re-reading familiar stories

**R T5:** to understand how story book language works and to use some formal elements when retelling stories

*without hair*

*story language*

*fruit of oak tree, like a nut*

*rhyming name*

*repetition in structure of story*

*question*

*answer*

*repeated speech*

*Chicken Licken doesn't know what happened, just that something fell from the sky; he makes a dramatic interpretation*

*typical character in traditional and fairy tales*

*went in the direction of*

*lots of use of initial 'l' phoneme*

*repetition in structure of story*

# CHICKEN LICKEN
*Extract 1*

ONE DAY, WHEN Chicken Licken was in the wood, an acorn fell from a tree on to his poor bald head. "Oh dear," thought Chicken Licken. "The sky is falling! I must go and tell the king."

So he left the wood and headed for the king's palace. On the way there he met Hen Len.

"Well, Hen Len," he said, "where are you going?"

"I'm going to the wood," said Hen Len.

"Oh, don't go there," said Chicken Licken, "for I was there and the sky fell on my poor bald head and I'm going to tell the king."

"Can I come with you?" asked Hen Len.

"Certainly," said Chicken Licken. So they both went off together to tell the king the sky was falling.

As they travelled along, they met Cock Lock. "Well, Cock Lock," said Hen Len, "where are you going?"

"I'm going to the wood," said Cock Lock.

"Oh, Cock Lock, don't go there, said Hen Len, "for Chicken Licken was there and the sky fell on his poor bald head and we're going to tell the king."

"May I come with you?" said Cock Lock.

"Certainly," said Chicken Licken.

So off they all went together to tell the king the sky was falling.

**R T7:** to use knowledge of familiar texts to re-enact or retell to others, recounting the main points in correct sequence

**R T12:** through guided and independent writing:
● to write labels or captions for pictures and drawings
● to write sentences to match pictures or sequences of pictures

# Chicken Licken

Traditional

*Extract 2*

## Background

This extract continues the Chicken Licken story. The children may anticipate the ending, but it should be read to emphasise tension and then surprise when the fox takes the unsuspecting animals to his den instead of going to see the king. In this story Fox Lox plays the part of the trickster. This tradition goes back to the medieval stories of Reynard the Fox which were popular in Europe from around 1150, and is a recurring theme in folk literature and children's stories, such as Roald Dahl's *Fantastic Mr Fox*.

## Shared reading and discussing the text

● Recap the story so far, then read this extract.

● Ask the children if the story ended as they expected. Compare it with the 'happy' ending in 'The Three Billy Goats Gruff' (page 78). Have they heard 'Chicken Licken' with a different ending? If so which ending do they prefer?

● Re-read the last sentence. What word is used to describe the way the fox ate the companions up? (*Gobbled.*) Does it create a picture of the way the fox ate? (Greedily and quickly.)

● Re-read the title and draw attention to the initial phoneme in *Chicken*. Ask the children if they can think of other words that begin with the same phoneme. Then give the children a list of words (*chair, china, sheep, chain* and so on) and ask them to indicate when they hear the odd one out.

● Fox Lox lives in a den; where do other animals live? What about a rabbit? A robin? Extend the children's knowledge by asking if they know other animal homes, such as a badger's sett.

## Activities

● Using a range of art materials, scraps of material and wool, help the children to make simple stick puppets of the characters in the story. The children can use the puppets as story props to practise retelling the story. Alternatively, fix small magnets to the back of cardboard characters and use these with a magnetic board.

● Provide a small group with a large sheet of paper on which you have drawn the route that Chicken Licken takes on the way to see the king. Include a path to the fox's den. Ask the children to draw the different characters that Chicken Licken meets on the way.

● In shared writing, write an alternative ending for the story. Perhaps Chicken Licken eventually gets to tell the king that the sky is falling down or perhaps he realises or is told that it was just an acorn after all. What might happen to the fox?

● Ask the children to retell the story, in pairs, onto tape. Encourage them to listen to their recording and share it with other children.

● In small groups, the children could play a rhyme game based on *-ox*. Gather a collection of items or pictures that rhyme with *fox*, for example box, socks, clocks, and some that do not rhyme with *fox*. Explain that one child will be Fox Lox and the rest of the group are other characters from the story. Tell the children that to avoid being caught by Fox Lox they need to pick an object that rhymes with his name and carry it past him. If the object rhymes he will not catch you, but if it doesn't he will try to catch you for his dinner.

● Make a story frieze together. Children working in pairs or a small group can create pictures of the characters. Write dialogue from the story in speech bubbles. Point out that it is only the words spoken by the characters that you write in the bubbles.

## Extension/further reading

Have a story exchange. Encourage the children to tell the story to someone at home in exchange for another story. Then ask the children to share the new stories with each other.

Try more cumulative patterned stories, such as *The Gingerbread Man* by Hugh Lupton (Barefoot Books), *The House That Jack Built* by Jenny Stow (Frances Lincoln) and *The Great Big Enormous Turnip* by Helen Oxenbury (Mammoth).

**R W1:** to understand and be able to rhyme through: recognising, exploring and working with rhyming patterns

**R W2:** knowledge of grapheme/phoneme correspondences through: hearing and identifying initial sounds in words

**R T7:** to use knowledge of familiar texts to re-enact or retell to others, recounting the main points in correct sequence

## CHICKEN LICKEN

*Extract 2*

A little while later they met Fox Lox. And Fox Lox said, "Where are you going?"

"Chicken Licken was in the wood and the sky fell on his poor bald head," said all the birds together, "and we're going to tell the king."

"Come with me," said Fox Lox, "and I will show you the way to the palace. The king will be delighted to see you."

They all followed Fox Lox until they came to a dark, dark hole in the edge of the hillside. "This is the way to the king's palace," said Fox Lox. So in went Chicken Licken, Hen Len, Cock Lock, Duck Luck, Drake Lake, Goose Loose and Turkey Lurkey, one after the other. But this was not the way to the king's palace, it was Fox Lox's den. And in no time at all Fox Lox had gobbled up every one of them, so they never saw the king to tell him that the sky was falling.

*time passing; story language*

*ominous; warning that something isn't right*

*name for a fox's home; shelter for a wild animal; others include:*
*lair*
*nest*
*burrow*
*sett*

*not a happy ending for characters we've been following*

*very pleased*

*'ox' rhymes include:*
*fox*
*box*
*and:*
*socks*
*clocks*
*locks*
*knocks*

*ate greedily, quickly*

**R T8:** to locate and read significant parts of the text, e.g. names of key characters, rhymes and chants

**R T9:** to be aware of story structures, e.g. actions/reactions, consequences, and the ways that stories are built up and concluded

**R T14:** to use experience of stories, poems and simple recounts as a basis for independent writing, e.g. retelling, substitution, extension, and through shared composition with adults

# What is the moon?
by Caroline Dunant

*Extracts 1 and 2*

## Background

These extracts are taken from the beginning and end of a contemporary story which uses a question and answer structure to depict a child's awe and wonder at the natural world and the different kinds of explanations parents can give. The text has a lovely, simple flow and some lines are in rhyming couplets, which provide a reassuring feel. The text can be used as a starting point for looking at space and the solar system; it can be linked with 'Rocket song' (page 90) and 'Take a Walk on a Rainbow' (page 108).

## Shared reading and discussing the text

● Ask the children if they have ever wondered what it is like on the moon. Has anyone seen the moon through a telescope? What does it look like? Has anyone seen pictures or television footage of the surface of the moon?

● Tell the children that you are going to read a story about a child who wonders what it is like on the moon. Read the extracts.

● Ask the children if they liked the story. Why or why not?

● Ask why the child asks a lot of questions and encourage the children to relate this to their own experience. What sorts of questions do they ask? Do they have brothers or sisters who ask their parents lots of questions?

● Encourage the children to imagine where the moon might 'go' when we cannot see it. Then provide some brief factual information about the phases of the moon. Consider what happens on a cloudy night – the clouds block the moon, the moon does not go behind the clouds).

● Re-read the story together, showing the children that the child's voice is given in italic. Why does the child think the moon is sad? Ask the children to reflect on times when they like being alone and other times when they don't and would rather have company.

## Activities

● On a large sheet of paper draw a circle to represent the moon and around it write out the last two lines of the story. Give a copy to each group and ask the children to draw on the moon all the things the child might do if she visited the moon for tea. If possible, listen to and observe the children collaborating as they decide what to draw.

● Take on the role of the moon. Give the children a couple of minutes to discuss what they would like to know about the moon, then let them ask questions which you answer in role. You could reverse this: in role as the moon, ask the children questions to find out what Earth is like.

● In shared or guided writing, write an additional episode for the story in which the child does go to the moon. Ask the children to decide whether she wants to return home or stay on the moon.

● Focus on the child imagining the moon as sad and lonely. Ask the children to think about things that can make them sad and things that make them happy. Provide a range of art and craft materials for the children to make either a sad or happy picture. Caption the children's artwork from their dictation, or encourage them to write captions independently.

● Help groups to write a story based on the question and answer format, for example 'What is the sun?', 'What are the stars?'.

## Extension/further reading

Display facts and pictures of the solar system. Suspend labelled model planets from the ceiling.

Other story books about the moon include: *Papa, Please Get the Moon For Me* by Eric Carle (Hamish Hamilton), *The Sea of Tranquility* by Mark Haddon and Christian Birmingham (Picture Lions), *Seven Ways to Catch the Moon* by MP Robertson (Frances Lincoln) and *Whatever Next!* by Jill Murphy (Macmillan).

R W6: to read on sight the 45 high-frequency words to be taught by the end of YR from Appendix List 1

# What is the moon?

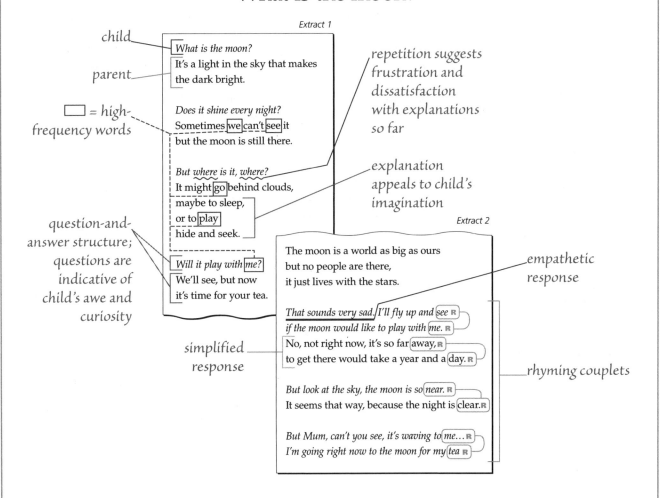

*Extract 1*

child

parent

▭ = high-frequency words

What is the moon?
It's a light in the sky that makes the dark bright.

Does it shine every night?
Sometimes we can't see it but the moon is still there.

repetition suggests frustration and dissatisfaction with explanations so far

But where is it, where?
It might go behind clouds, maybe to sleep, or to play hide and seek.

explanation appeals to child's imagination

*Extract 2*

question-and-answer structure; questions are indicative of child's awe and curiosity

Will it play with me?
We'll see, but now it's time for your tea.

The moon is a world as big as ours but no people are there, it just lives with the stars.

empathetic response

That sounds very sad, I'll fly up and see R
if the moon would like to play with me. R
No, not right now, it's so far away, R
to get there would take a year and a day. R

simplified response

But look at the sky, the moon is so near. R
It seems that way, because the night is clear. R

rhyming couplets

But Mum, can't you see, it's waving to me... R
I'm going right now to the moon for my tea R

R T12: through guided and independent writing: to write labels or captions for pictures and drawings

R T14: to use experience of stories, as a basis for independent writing, e.g. retelling, substitution, extension, and through shared composition with adults

# Down by the Cool of the Pool
by Tony Mitton

## Background

This extract is from a fun story with a cumulative structure that makes it ideal for children to join in with, as the words are quickly committed to memory. Humour is derived from sound and movement, for example the hilarious images of a wiggling pig and a dancing frog. This extract links to other animal texts in this book: 'Cats' (page 60), 'Let's Look at Animals' (page 68), 'Farmyard Hullabaloo' (page 88) and the cumulative rhyme 'Old Macdonald had a farm' (page 102).

## Shared reading and discussing the text

● Prior to reading the text, display a selection of humorous picture books (see below for suggested titles). Then introduce the text by telling the children you are going to read from a story about some animals by a pool on a hot day. Ask the children if they like paddling and playing in a pool when the weather is hot. Is it nice and *cool*?

● Read the text, then ask the children what words they would use to describe the poem. (*Funny, happy, humorous.*) What happens at the end? (All the animals jump in the pool.)

● Pick out some of the lines that are repeated in the story. Ask the children if they can remember them. Highlight them on the text.

● Re-read the last section. Talk about the noises the animals make which show that they are having fun (*Ooh, Whooop, Wheeee, Oh, ha-ha-hee*). Draw attention to the bold word *in* in the final line, re-reading to show how it contrasts with *down by* and helps an expressive reading.

● Re-read the text together and ask the children to continue on their own whenever you stop.

## Activities

● Use a range of craft materials to produce simple animal masks. Encourage the children to wear their masks and improvise a retelling of the story. The masks could also be worn in subsequent readings of the poem. You could also allocate lines so that, for example, children wearing pig masks can read Pig's speech.

● Re-read sections of the text to draw attention to words that describe the animals' movements (*dance, flap* and so on). Ask the children to think about words that might be used to describe other animals. Include some familiar creatures and more unusual ones to challenge the children, for example *snake slithers; mouse scurries; cat stalks; bird hops; ant crawls.* Make a list of the suggestions.

● Using the format of the text as a model, compose more lines with the children, such as *Fish came to see. 'I can dance too. But not like you. I can splash.'* Ask the children to choose animals and movement words from your list.

● On the board, write the sentences *I can flap, I can wiggle, I can dance.* Underneath, write the unfinished sentence, *I can…* Read the sentences and ask the children to help you complete the unfinished sentence. What sorts of movement can they make? For example, dance, skip, hop, run.

● On pieces of card, write the sentences *I can flap, I can wiggle* and *I can dance.* Produce a set of picture cards with a frog, duck and pig. Ask the children to match the statements to the correct animals.

● Focus on the rhyme family -*ool.* As a class or group, generate a list of words to rhyme with *cool* and *pool,* for example *stool, school, rule, fool, tool.*

## Extension/further reading

Have a cool pool party. Ask the children to bring in their favourite toy animals to join the party. Invitations can be sent to the animals (see 'Party invitation', page 30). Alternatively, the children might receive an invitation from Frog inviting them to the party.

Read the full text of *Down by the Cool of the Pool.* Other suggestions are *Giraffes Can't Dance* by Giles Andreae and Guy Parker-Rees (Orchard), *The Dance of the Dinosaurs* by Colin and Jacqui Hawkins (Picture Lions), *Commotion in the Ocean* and *Rumble in the Jungle* by Giles Andreae and David Wojtowycz (Orchard).

**R W1:** to understand and be able to rhyme through:
● recognising, exploring and working with rhyming patterns, e.g. learning nursery rhymes
● extending these patterns by analogy, generating new and invented words in speech and spelling

**R W6:** to read on sight the 45 high-frequency words to be taught by the end of YR from Appendix List 1

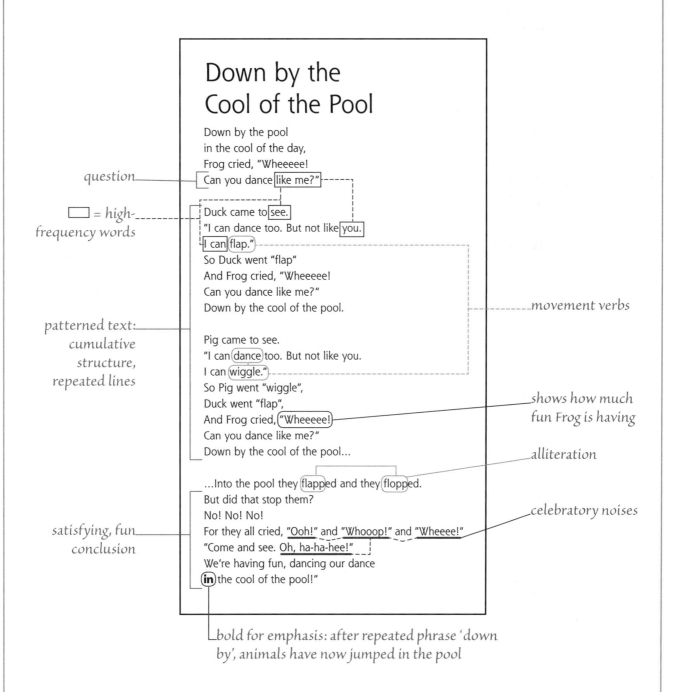

# Down by the Cool of the Pool

Down by the pool
in the cool of the day,
Frog cried, "Wheeeee!
Can you dance like me?"

Duck came to see.
"I can dance too. But not like you.
I can flap."
So Duck went "flap"
And Frog cried, "Wheeeee!
Can you dance like me?"
Down by the cool of the pool.

Pig came to see.
"I can dance too. But not like you.
I can wiggle."
So Pig went "wiggle",
Duck went "flap",
And Frog cried, "Wheeeee!
Can you dance like me?"
Down by the cool of the pool...

...Into the pool they flapped and they flopped.
But did that stop them?
No! No! No!
For they all cried, "Ooh!" and "Whooop!" and "Wheeee!"
"Come and see. Oh, ha-ha-hee!"
We're having fun, dancing our dance
**in** the cool of the pool!"

*question*

☐ *= high-frequency words*

*patterned text: cumulative structure, repeated lines*

*movement verbs*

*shows how much fun Frog is having*

*alliteration*

*celebratory noises*

*satisfying, fun conclusion*

*bold for emphasis: after repeated phrase 'down by', animals have now jumped in the pool*

**R T7:** to use knowledge of familiar texts to re-enact or retell to others, recounting the main points in correct sequence

**R T8:** to locate and read significant parts of the text, e.g. names of key characters, chants

**R T10:** to re-read stories with predictable and repeated patterns

# Farmyard Hullabaloo

by Giles Andreae   *Extracts 1–3*

## Background
This text uses the form of a narrative poem to let farm animals introduce characteristics of themselves, particularly their noises and movements. It has the same time structure as 'Five Busy Farmers' (page 96) and can be used alongside it. It also links to the other animal texts 'Let's Look at Animals' (page 68), 'Down by the Cool of the Pool' (page 86) and 'Old Macdonald had a farm' (page 102).

## Shared reading and discussing the text
● Place plastic models of the animals mentioned in the rhyme next to a farm play mat.
● Focus on day and night. Ask the children what wakes them up in the morning. What sorts of things do they do during the day? Choose a couple of the daytime activities and ask the children to mime them. Use prompt questions to encourage them to extend their mime. Then ask them what sorts of routines they have at bedtime.
● Read the title. Discuss what a *hullabaloo* is. Tell the children to listen out for words that describe noises as you read the text.
● Read the first extract. Pause to allow the children to 'wake up' each of the plastic farm animals and arrange them on the mat.
● Read extracts 2 and 3, and make sure the children understand unfamiliar vocabulary such as *clamber, snuffle* and *fleece*. Establish the time frame of the story.
● Ask the children if they have a favourite farm animal and encourage them to give reasons for their choice. What noises and movements do they make?
● Re-read the text, with the sub-headings covered. Pause to allow the children to predict the rhyming words and answer the 'riddles' of the animals presenting themselves.

## Activities
● Let the children play 'Snap' using cards of the animals in the text (pig, rooster, sheepdog, cow, sheep). The set of cards could also include a frog and duck from 'Down by the Cool of the Pool' (page 86). The cards should show the picture of the animal and its name.
● Re-read extracts 1 and 2, then, in shared or guided writing, make a lift-the-flap book of animal noises. The children should draw a different farm animal for each page of the book. Make flaps to cover the picture. On the flaps write the words: *I moo! What am I?* and so on. Each animal can then be revealed during reading. Read the book in shared reading.
● Play a tape or CD of animal noises/sound effects and talk about which animal is making the noise. Then give the children a set of animal cards or model animals. Play the tape again. After each sound is played the children should decide which animal made the noise and arrange their set of animals in the order they hear them.
● Make a class display called 'Farmyard Hullabaloo'. Use children's paintings of farm animals and include text from the story, for example *Mooing and chewing are what I like doing; I love looking after my piglets.*
● Compose another verse for the poem about a different animal. Prepare a text with blanks which can be completed in shared writing. For example:

### Cat
I may look as though I am sleeping
By the fire inside the farmhouse,
But the farmer needs me to help him
Catch the odd rat and _____.

## Extension/further reading
Make a class collage of night-time and daytime activities. The collage can be made from children's artwork as well as pictures from catalogues, magazines and brochures.
    If possible, take the children to visit a farm.
    Suggestions for animal-noise and day-to-night stories are *Noisy Farm* by Rod Campbell (Picture Puffins), *Goodnight Owl* by Pat Hutchins (Jonathan Cape), *Peace at Last* by Jill Murphy (Macmillan Children's Books) and *Lullabyhullaballoo!* by Mick Inkpen (Hodder).

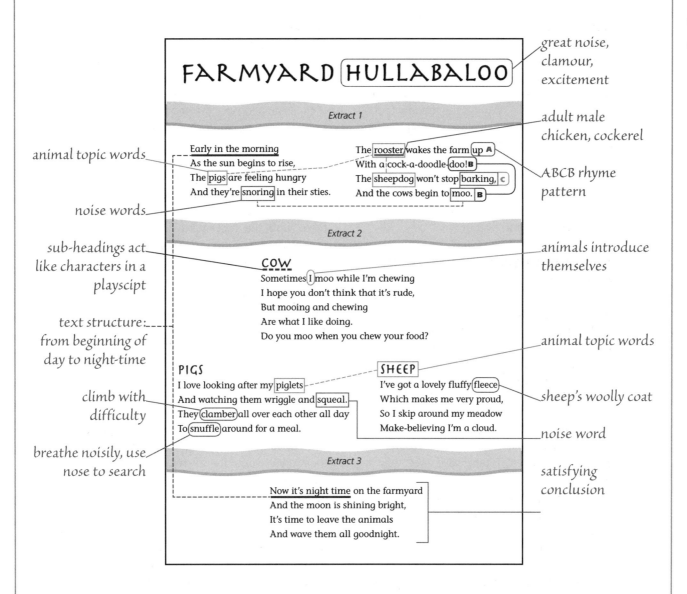

great noise, clamour, excitement

adult male chicken, cockerel

ABCB rhyme pattern

animal topic words

noise words

sub-headings act like characters in a playscipt

text structure: from beginning of day to night-time

climb with difficulty

breathe noisily, use nose to search

animals introduce themselves

animal topic words

sheep's woolly coat

noise word

satisfying conclusion

**FARMYARD HULLABALOO**

Extract 1

Early in the morning
As the sun begins to rise,
The pigs are feeling hungry
And they're snoring in their sties.

The rooster wakes the farm up A
With a cock-a-doodle-doo! B
The sheepdog won't stop barking, C
And the cows begin to moo. B

Extract 2

COW
Sometimes I moo while I'm chewing
I hope you don't think that it's rude,
But mooing and chewing
Are what I like doing.
Do you moo when you chew your food?

PIGS
I love looking after my piglets
And watching them wriggle and squeal.
They clamber all over each other all day
To snuffle around for a meal.

SHEEP
I've got a lovely fluffy fleece
Which makes me very proud,
So I skip around my meadow
Make-believing I'm a cloud.

Extract 3

Now it's night time on the farmyard
And the moon is shining bright,
It's time to leave the animals
And wave them all goodnight.

# Rocket song

by Barbara Ireson

## Background

This is the first in a group of poems that focus on the subject of travel and transport (see 'Early in the morning', page 92 and 'The Train Journey', page 94). It continues the theme of space introduced in 'What is the moon?' (page 84). Its onomatopoeic qualities, strong rhythm and regular rhyme scheme make it fun to read aloud and good for encouraging prediction. The poem is a mini story with a neat narrative structure: beginning – the take off; the landing on the moon; the end of the journey, after re-entering the Earth's orbit.

## Shared reading and discussing the text

● Prior to reading the selection of texts about travel and transport, set up a stimulus display with pictures of different types of transport and destinations, for example a picture of a rocket and the moon; a boat and a tropical island. Accompany the pictures with written questions, for example *How would you travel to the moon? How would you travel to school?*
● Using the Internet (for example, www. nasa.gov) and other sources, gather a range of resources about the moon and space travel.
● Ask the children if they have ever seen a rocket. Where did they see it? Have they seen a rocket or other spaceship in a film?
● Ask the children if they have ever imagined what it would be like to travel to the moon. Explain that 'Rocket song' is about a journey to the moon and back.
● Recite the poem and ask the children if they liked it. What did they like about it?
● Ask volunteers to tell you the story of the poem. What is happening in each verse?
● Ask the children if they can think of any actions to accompany the poem. (For example, pointing high for taking off; clapping and waving for *cheers and claps and handshakes*.)
● Explore with the children why everyone cheers when the capsule splashes down. (The astronauts have arrived back safely; the mission has been successful; space travel is an exciting achievement.)

## Activities

● Use the poem's narrative structure to create a drama. The children can mime making preparations for the space journey and exploring their new environment on arrival at their destination on the moon. A movement from Holst's *Planet Suite* might be used to create atmosphere. After splashdown, hot-seating could be used to encourage the children to describe their imaginary experiences.
● Help the children to make model rockets using plastic bottles and card, and decorate them with the movement phrases from the text: *Boom off! Zoom off! Drop down!* and so on. Draw attention to onset and rime and repeated words as you write. Suspend the rockets from the ceiling, with the planets from 'What is the moon?' if appropriate.
● Focus on the adverbs *up* and *down*: a rocket travels up into space and then splashes down into the ocean. Talk about other things that go up and down, for example an escalator, lift, aeroplane, a person jumping. Make a group display entitled 'Things that go up and down'. Ask the children to draw one of the things mentioned and encourage them to caption their own work, for example *An aeroplane goes up and down, A kangaroo jumps up and down.*

## Extension/further reading

Begin a collection of models and pictures of different kinds of transport to produce a museum exhibition. Word-process labels for the artefacts. Guide the children to experiment with font, style, size and colour.

If possible, visit a museum to see space exhibits, for example at the Science Museum in London or National Space Centre in Leicester, or show some video footage of the 1969 moon landing.

Look at different genres on the topic, for example *Poems About Space* compiled by Brian Moses (Hodder Wayland), *Whatever Next!* by Jill Murphy (Macmillan), *1969 – A Year to Remember* (Telstar Video).

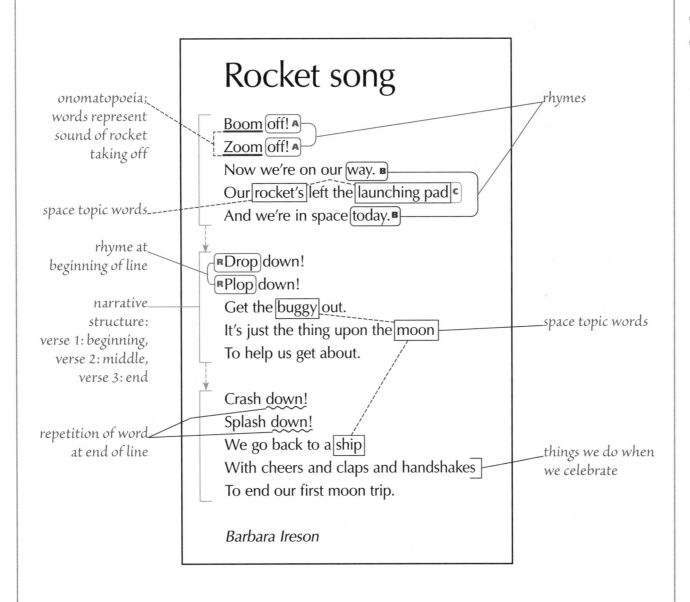

# Rocket song

onomatopoeia;
words represent
sound of rocket
taking off

rhymes

Boom off! **A**
Zoom off! **A**
Now we're on our way. **B**
Our rocket's left the launching pad **c**
And we're in space today. **B**

space topic words

rhyme at
beginning of line

**R**Drop down!
**R**Plop down!
Get the buggy out.
It's just the thing upon the moon
To help us get about.

narrative
structure:
verse 1: beginning,
verse 2: middle,
verse 3: end

space topic words

repetition of word
at end of line

Crash down!
Splash down!
We go back to a ship
With cheers and claps and handshakes
To end our first moon trip.

things we do when
we celebrate

*Barbara Ireson*

**R W10:** new words from their reading and shared experiences

**R W11:** to make collections of personal interest or significant words and words linked to particular topics

**R T12:** through guided and independent writing: to write labels or captions for pictures and drawings

# Early in the morning by Barbara Ireson

## Background
This poem links to the other transport poems in this section ('Rocket song', page 90 and 'The Train Journey', page 94). The vocabulary will be challenging for young children, but the patterned text is highly predictable and the onomatopoeic words that describe the different sounds made by the vehicles provide an opportunity to experiment with sound.

## Shared reading and discussing the text
● Before reading the text display a collection of model vehicles, including a train, boat, bus and aeroplane.
● Discuss the different places you might visit if you were travelling by aeroplane, boat, bus… Use the toy vehicles in posing questions, for example *Which one of these would you use to go abroad on holiday?*
● Check the children's understanding of vocabulary associated with transport, for example *What do we call a person who flies an aeroplane?*
● Read the poem to the children. Then re-read it, encouraging the children to follow the text and join in with the refrain.
● Identify the onomatopoeic words, such as *clickety clack*. Discuss what is making the noises suggested by them (train wheels on the track, propellers turning and so on). Practise playing with ways of saying the phrases to make the train, go faster and slower.
● Highlight the words *railway* and *seaside* and see if anyone can find smaller words in them. Can the children find another word like this? (*Airport*.)

## Activities
● On strips of card, write out the second line of each verse. Highlight the noun in a different colour. Make picture cards of the corresponding vehicles. Ask the children to match the sentence to the correct picture. Alternatively, cards can show just the names of the vehicles. Models can be used instead of pictures, if preferred. For more able children, you could write out the

third lines too, and encourage them to match the vehicles with their operators (train and driver and so on).
● Ask the children to paint their favourite type of vehicle (or allocate a vehicle to each group). Encourage them to paint it in the context given in the poem (trains at the station, boats at the seaside and so on). Use the pictures to create a wall frieze. Label the display, using appropriate lines from the poem as captions.
● Play 'Kim's Game', using a collection of model vehicles on a tray. Show the children the collection for 30 seconds. Ask them to close their eyes while you take one model away. When they open their eyes, ask them to say which one has been taken away. The game can be made easier or more difficult using fewer or more vehicles.
● In shared writing, compose another verse for the poem. Ask the children to think of other vehicles and where they would 'live', for example racing cars down at the racetrack, taxis down at the taxi rank.
● Help the children to experiment with a range of percussion instruments to reproduce the sounds of the different vehicles. Accompany a reading of the poem with the instruments.

## Extension/further reading
Read and listen to a variety of poems about transport and journeys, for example versions of 'The Wheels on the Bus'. Talk to the children about their favourites and combine them to make a class book. Use the children's illustrations to accompany the poems.

Make available a collection of picture books that feature different forms of transport, such as *Travel and Transport Then and Now* (Usborne), *On Wheels* (Moonlight Publishing), *Cars, Boats, Trains, and Planes* (Picture Lions). Encourage the children to browse through the books. Direct their attention to the pictures as sources of information, asking prompt questions (for example, *Where does the driver sit? Why does the driver sit there?*) to encourage them to look with attention.

**R W6:** to read on sight the 45 high-frequency words to be taught by the end of YR from Appendix List 1

**R W10:** new words from their reading and shared experiences

**R W11:** to make collections of personal interest or significant words and words linked to particular topics

*each type of vehicle has a 'home'/context*

# Early in the morning

*☐ = high-frequency words*

Come down to the station early in the morning,
See all the railway trains standing in a row.
See all the drivers starting up the engines,
Clickety click and clickety clack,
Off they go!

*repeated 'cl' blend*

Come down to the garage early in the morning,
See all the buses standing in a row.
See all the drivers starting up the engines,
Rumble, rumble, rumble, rumble,
Off they go!

*onomatopoeia: sound of train wheels moving on tracks, engines turning over, water slapping against boats, engines getting up to speed*

*〰 = patterned text: same structure is used each verse; highly predictable*

Come down to the seaside early in the morning,
See all the motor-boats floating in a row.
See all the drivers starting up the engines,
Splishing, splishing, sploshing, sploshing,
Off they go!

*repeated 'spl' cluster*

Come down to the airport early in the morning,
See all the aeroplanes standing in a row.
See all the pilots starting up the engines,
Whirring, whirring, whirring, whirring,
Off they go!

*where aircraft land and take off; where passengers go to catch a plane*

*Barbara Ireson*

*people who fly planes*

**R T2:** to use a variety of cues when reading: knowledge of the story and its context, and awareness of how it should make sense grammatically

**R T12:** through guided and independent writing: to write labels or captions for pictures and drawings

**R T14:** to use experience of poems as a basis for independent writing, e.g. extension, and through shared composition with adults

# The Train Journey
by Brenda Williams

## Background

This is a rhythmic text featuring rhyme and repetition. The unusual layout reinforces this and encourages pause and prediction. The poem can provide a stimulus for work on journeys, real and imagined, as well as extending the children's responses to language rhythms.

## Shared reading and discussing the text

● Gather a collection of pictures showing train travel in the past and present.

● Prior to reading the poem, discuss the children's experiences of train journeys. It is likely that many children will not have travelled by train, but most will have seen one. Their knowledge of steam trains may come from stories and television programmes such as *Thomas the Tank Engine*. Talk about the sound that the train wheels make on the track.

● Read the poem to the children, emphasising the rhythm to imitate the train travelling at speed and slowing down as it comes into the station.

● Direct the children's attention to the layout of the poem and explain how it helped you to read it.

● Read the poem together. The children could be seated in two rows of pairs with a central aisle as if in a railway carriage, bringing out the drama in the poem.

## Activities

● Tell the children a journey story. Ask them to imagine they are going by train on an exciting holiday. They are packing their suitcases, but after they have packed their clothes and wash-kits, they can only take one special toy. Ask them to draw the toy. Share the drawings and encourage the children to talk about their reasons for choosing that item.

● In small groups, help the children to devise a musical accompaniment for the different stages of the journey. Re-read the poem, encouraging the children to listen out for sounds that can be represented.

● Continue the journey story by describing the arrival at the destination. Through role-play, the children can explore what they might do on arrival at the destination. Then model writing postcards in shared writing. Using a large blank postcard, write a name and address on the right-hand side, drawing attention to writing conventions as appropriate. Ask the children what message they want to put on the card. Select and scribe one of their suggestions, noting the conventions for the salutation and signing off. Have some blank and picture postcards available in the writing or imaginative play area for the children to write on.

● Working on initial consonants, re-read the first two lines of the poem. Draw attention to the repetition of *back,* emphasising the *b*. Ask the children to listen and identify the odd one out from a word list such as *bread, orange, butter, biscuit, banana*. The activity can be extended to include words with the *p* phoneme, for example *bin, ball, pot, bottle*. The task can help to identify children with possible short-term hearing impairments. You could make a game using pictures of the objects (cut out from magazines and catalogues), asking the children to indicate which picture is the odd one out – for example, does not start with the phoneme *b*. The process can be repeated for the consonant phoneme *t* from *top*.

● Focus on the rhyme families *-ack* and *-ick*. Generate real and imaginary rhyming words and work with a small group to tell a story that includes as many of them as possible (for example, *Jack, back, sack, black, track, pack*).

## Extension/further reading

Set up a train track with a selection of model trains in the play area.

Further reading on trains can include *Let's go by Train* in Heinemann's *Little Nippers* series, the *Thomas the Tank Engine* series (Heinemann), *The Train Ride* by June Crebbin (Walker Books), *Oi! Get Off Our Train* by John Burningham (Red Fox) and 'From a Railway Carriage' in *A Child's Garden of Verses* by Robert Louis Stevenson.

R **W2:** knowledge of grapheme/phoneme correspondences through:
● hearing and identifying initial sounds in words
● reading letters that represent the sounds *a-z*

R **W4:** to link sound and spelling patterns by: discriminating 'onsets' from 'rimes' in speech and spelling

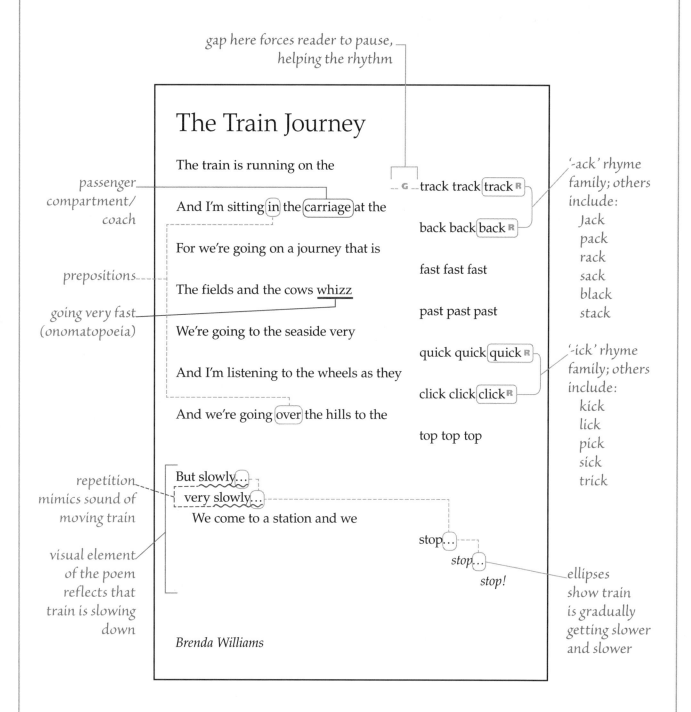

*gap here forces reader to pause, helping the rhythm*

## The Train Journey

The train is running on the

And I'm sitting in the carriage at the

For we're going on a journey that is

The fields and the cows whizz

We're going to the seaside very

And I'm listening to the wheels as they

And we're going over the hills to the

But slowly...
  very slowly...
    We come to a station and we

stop...
  stop...
    stop!

*Brenda Williams*

G track track track R

back back back R

fast fast fast

past past past

quick quick quick R

click click click R

top top top

*passenger compartment/ coach*

*prepositions*

*going very fast (onomatopoeia)*

*repetition mimics sound of moving train*

*visual element of the poem reflects that train is slowing down*

*'-ack' rhyme family; others include:*
  *Jack*
  *pack*
  *rack*
  *sack*
  *black*
  *stack*

*'-ick' rhyme family; others include:*
  *kick*
  *lick*
  *pick*
  *sick*
  *trick*

*ellipses show train is gradually getting slower and slower*

R **T11:** through shared writing:
● to understand that writing can be used for a range of purposes
● to understand how writing is formed directionally, a word at a time
● to understand how letters are formed and used to spell words

R **T15:** to use writing to communicate in a variety of ways, incorporating it into play and everyday classroom life, e.g. recounting their own experiences, labels, greeting cards, letters

# Five Busy Farmers

### Background

'Five Busy Farmers' is a counting rhyme with a daytime-to-night-time structure and simple rhyme scheme. Links can be made with the other counting rhymes ('Five Ducks Five', page 46 and 'Monsters', page 58) and with 'Farmyard Hullabaloo' (page 88), which also uses the time structure of one day.

### Shared reading and discussing the text

● Before reading, display sets of pictures showing traditional and modern methods of farming.

● Talk to the children about their knowledge of farming. What sort of animals are kept? What crops are grown? What jobs need to be done? Explain that they are going to learn a counting rhyme about five farmers and how they spend their day working on the farm.

● Read the text to the children, making sure they understand unfamiliar vocabulary, such as *chores*, *plough* and *pens*. Ask them what time of day it is at the start of the poem. How do they know? What time is it at the end?

● Re-read the rhyme, pausing to allow the children to supply the number of the farmer you are up to and the rhyming words.

### Activities

● Choose five children to be the farmers and to mime actions to represent the chores – milking the cow and so on. These children can perform as the rest of the class recite the rhyme. Repeat the activity with different children taking on the roles of the farmers.

● Give the children a copy of the text each. Recite the poem together, asking the children to indicate when they hear a rhyme. Get them to look at their copies of the poem and guide them to find the rhyming words in the text. Ask them to colour the rhyming pair, using a different colour for each rhyme.

● With prompts from the children, make a list of the animals mentioned in the story. Extend the list by asking the children to suggest other farm animals. Add some challenges, for example by asking them if they know names for male and female animals or adult and young (horse: mare, stallion; foal or pony). Compile a list of topic words and display it where the children can refer to it.

● Re-read the last verse and focus on the *-ed* rhyme family. Brainstorm some other words (real or made-up) that rhyme with *red* and *bed*.

● Ask the children to paint the five farmers' actions. Include an early morning scene, and a night-time scene showing the farmers tucked in bed and sleeping. Ask the children to choose lines from the text to accompany their depictions.

● Produce an audio tape or CD of daytime and night-time noises. (Libraries often have collections of sound effects CDs.) Play the tape and talk about which noises can be heard during the day and which can be heard at night. Re-read the poem and discuss what noises might be heard at each stage of the story.

### Extension/further reading

In PE, consolidate learning of ordinal numbers. Give the children number cards from 1 to 5. Tell the children to move around the hall and on the stop signal walk to join with other children to make a number line from 1 to 5. Check that all groups are in the correct order and reinforce the use of *first, second, third...*

Good poetry collections and story books on this topic include *Five Little Monkeys* (Dutton Children's Books), *Round and Round the Garden* by Ian Beck and Sarah Williams (OUP), *1 2 3 to the Zoo* by Eric Carle (Puffin Books) and *Cockatoos* by Quentin Blake (Red Fox).

**R W1:** to understand and be able to rhyme through:
● recognising, exploring and working with rhyming patterns, e.g. learning nursery rhymes
● extending these patterns by analogy, generating new and invented words in speech and spelling

**R W4:** to link sound and spelling patterns by: using knowledge of rhyme to identify families of rhyming CVC words

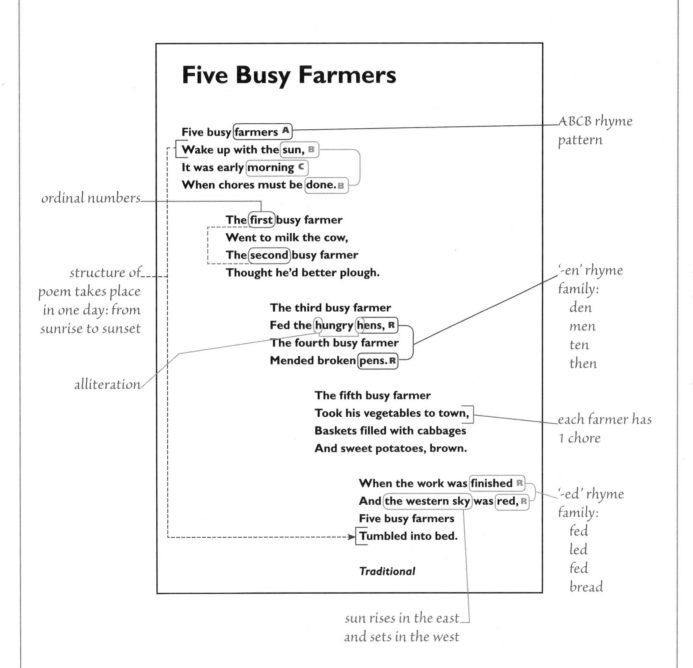

# Five Busy Farmers

Five busy farmers **A**
Wake up with the sun, **B**
It was early morning **C**
When chores must be done. **B**

The first busy farmer
Went to milk the cow,
The second busy farmer
Thought he'd better plough.

The third busy farmer
Fed the hungry hens, **R**
The fourth busy farmer
Mended broken pens. **R**

The fifth busy farmer
Took his vegetables to town,
Baskets filled with cabbages
And sweet potatoes, brown.

When the work was finished **R**
And the western sky was red, **R**
Five busy farmers
Tumbled into bed.

*Traditional*

ABCB rhyme pattern

ordinal numbers

structure of poem takes place in one day: from sunrise to sunset

alliteration

'-en' rhyme family:
den
men
ten
then

each farmer has 1 chore

'-ed' rhyme family:
fed
led
fed
bread

sun rises in the east and sets in the west

**R T3:** to re-read a text to provide context cues to help read unfamiliar words

**R T10:** to re-read and recite stories and rhymes with predictable and repeated patterns and experiment with similar rhyming patterns

# One is a lion

by Brenda Williams

### Background

This is a counting poem in rhyming couplets. It can support the development of phonological awareness and encourage prediction. It provides an accessible model for stimulating group and independent writing. It includes colour words and can be read with other texts about colour – 'What is pink?' (page 100) and 'Take a Walk on a Rainbow' (page 108). It might also be used as a stimulus for exploring colour and camouflage in the animal kingdom or alongside other counting rhymes, for example 'Monsters' (page 58).

### Shared reading and discussing the text

● Display a collection of pictures and books that focus on animals' colour and camouflage. Try to include colour images of the animals mentioned in the text.

● Discuss favourite colours. Encourage the children to talk about why they prefer some colours to others. Ask whether colours can affect the way we feel. Show some colour samples and think about the feelings that the colours evoke. Colour can also have cultural significance and different cultural meanings need to be appreciated.

● Read the text, checking the children's understanding about concepts of print (where to begin, how to follow the line and so on). Be aware of the punctuation as you read, the full stops causing you to pause after each couplet.

● Pick out the colour words and look at images of the animals mentioned. Draw attention to the different shades a frog can be: some dark and almost brown, others acidic green or almost yellow. Notice that a robin has a red breast. What other colours do the children see in the picture of a robin?

● Re-read the text, pausing to allow the children to supply the end rhyme in the second line of each couplet.

### Activities

● Use the text as a model for creating a group poem. You might supply your own first lines of couplets and ask the children to suggest rhyming words. For example, One is a brown puppy full of fun, Two is a black cat lying in the… Draw attention to high-frequency words, such as is, and to the number and colour words.

● Ask groups of children to work together to use sponges and different shades of colour to make large pictures of the animals in the text (for example, have different shades of green available for the green frog). Show the children what happens when green is mixed with a bit of white or a bit of blue. Use the pictures to create a wall frieze incorporating phrases from the text. Ask the children to help you order the animals correctly, using the number words as clues.

● Make a wall chart of colour words. On a large sheet of paper make some blocks of colour. Ask the children to help you label the blocks, and as you write, draw attention to the structure of the words (initial, medial and final phonemes). Display the chart in the classroom for the children's reference.

● Ask the children to bring in different-coloured carrier bags from home. Classify the carrier bags according to their dominant colours. Make a wall display and label it with the colour words, for example These bags are different shades of RED.

● In shared writing, show the children how they can make a chart to present easy-to-read information about their favourite colours, for example a tally chart or bar graph.

### Extension/further reading

Explore colour and camouflage in the animal kingdom. Watch an early learning video, such as Dorling Kindersley's Animal Disguises.

Other texts using animal colours include Brown Bear, Brown Bear, What Do You See? and Polar Bear, Polar Bear, What Do You Hear? by Bill Martin, Jr and Eric Carle; Eric Carle's The Mixed-Up Chameleon (all Picture Puffins), and Touch and Feel Animal Colours (Dorling Kindersley).

**R W4:** to link sound and spelling patterns by: discriminating 'onsets' from 'rimes' in speech and spelling

**R W6:** to read on sight the 45 high-frequency words to be taught by the end of YR from Appendix List 1

**R T1:** through shared reading: to track the text in the right order, left to right, top to bottom; pointing while reading/telling a story, and making one-to-one correspondences between written and spoken words

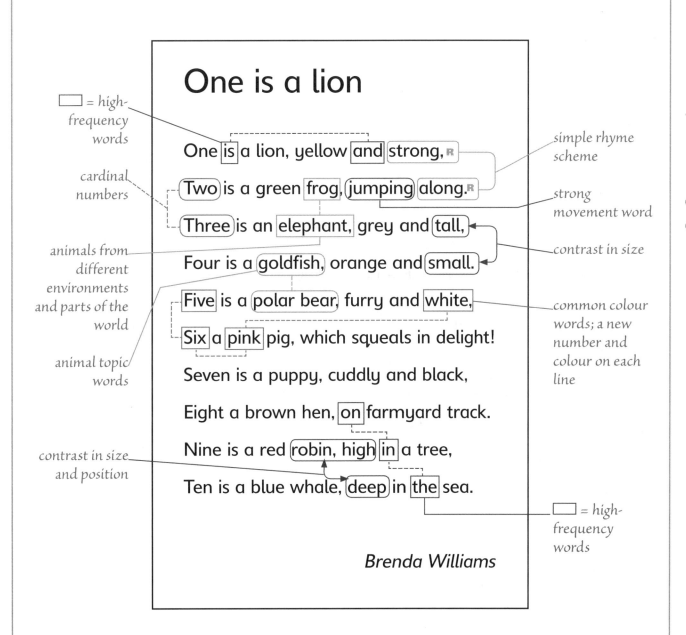

☐ = high-frequency words

cardinal numbers

animals from different environments and parts of the world

animal topic words

contrast in size and position

# One is a lion

One is a lion, yellow and strong, ®

Two is a green frog, jumping along. ®

Three is an elephant, grey and tall,

Four is a goldfish, orange and small.

Five is a polar bear, furry and white,

Six a pink pig, which squeals in delight!

Seven is a puppy, cuddly and black,

Eight a brown hen, on farmyard track.

Nine is a red robin, high in a tree,

Ten is a blue whale, deep in the sea.

*Brenda Williams*

simple rhyme scheme

strong movement word

contrast in size

common colour words; a new number and colour on each line

☐ = high-frequency words

**R T10:** to re-read and recite stories and rhymes with predictable and repeated patterns and experiment with similar rhyming patterns

**R T11:** through shared writing: to understand how letters are formed and used to spell words

# What is pink?

by Christina Rossetti

### Background

This is a classic lyrical poem written in the mid-19th century. The text contains some challenging vocabulary but it rewards re-reading. It evokes striking visual images and lends itself to creative exploration through art and craft activities. This text can be linked to other question and answer poems such as 'Goldilocks and the three bears' (page 22), or texts about colour such as 'One is a lion' (page 98) and 'Take a Walk on a Rainbow' (page 108).

### Shared reading and discussing the text

● To help the children's understanding, gather a collection of the items that are mentioned in the poem (or pictures of them).
● Read the title and ask the children to suggest what they think the poem will be about. What things do they know that are pink? What other colours can they name? If appropriate, extend their range of known colours by discriminating shades of colour, such as crimson and scarlet.
● Encourage the children to listen carefully as you read, and think about the pictures that the poem creates. Some children might like to close their eyes to help imagine the scenes.
● Explain unfamiliar words before re-reading, allowing the children to supply rhymes.
● Re-read the line *What is green? the grass is green*. Draw attention to the repeated initial *g*. Ask the children to suggest objects that begin with *g*, then other objects that are green.
● Consider whether colours can have different meanings, for example traffic lights; red and blue to denote hot and cold; blue lights for emergency vehicles; green cross for pharmacy.
● Re-read the poem to increase the children's appreciation of the text.

### Activities

● Ask the children to draw or paint images that are suggested to them by the poem. Then use found objects, photographs, sound effects (such as sounds of a water fountain) and children's artwork to make a multimedia display of images from the poem. Prepare lines from the poem for completion in shared writing, for example *What is red? a poppy's ___ In its barley ___* and include these in the display.
● Ask the children to agree on a choice of one of the colours from the poem and find a colour sample to match (for example, a red T-shirt, an orange or a piece cut from a magazine). Take the colour sample with you and the children on a walk around the school grounds. See how many objects can be found that match that colour. Ask a more able group of children to record the objects (in writing or pictorially) in notebooks. Or digital photographs could be taken and included in a Powerpoint presentation along with appropriate captions.
● In groups of three, let the children practise performing the poem. Ask one child to read the questions (the first half of a line), one the answers (the second half) and the third the contexts (the next line).
● Write two additional lines for the poem, choosing a colour not used in the poem. For example, *What is black? Night is black / Creeping through the curtain's crack*.
● Focus on the *-ink* rhyme family from *pink*. Can the children see the common spelling pattern in *pink* and *brink*? Encourage them to suggest other words that rhyme with *pink*, for example *ink, link, rink, sink, stink, think*.

### Extension/further reading

Gather a collection of books on flowers. Let the children search for pictures of poppies, violets and roses and for flowers coloured, for example, white, blue, yellow and orange. Provide a sheet with outline drawings of labelled flowers, for example bluebell, rose, daffodil. Ask the children to find out the colours of the flowers and colour them accordingly.

Look at other Rossetti poems in *Sing-Song: A Nursery Rhyme Book* (Dover Publications). Other suitable books on colour are *White Rabbit's Colour Book* by Alan Baker (Kingfisher), *Elmer's Colours* by David McKee (Andersen Press) and *Strawberries are red* by Petr Horacek (Walker Books).

**R W2:** knowledge of grapheme/phoneme correspondences through: hearing and identifying initial sounds in words

lyrical poem

# What is pink?

What is pink? a rose is pink R
By the fountain's brink. R
What is red? a poppy's red
In its barley bed.
What is blue? the sky is blue R
Where the clouds float thro'. R
What is white? a swan is white
Sailing in the light.
What is yellow? pears are yellow,
Rich and ripe and mellow.
What is green? the grass is green,
With small flowers between.
What is violet? clouds are violet
In the summer twilight.
What is orange? why, an orange,
Just an orange!

*Christina Rossetti*

colours; each one represented by a scenic image

cereal crop – poppies are often seen in its fields

question

answer

mature, ready for eating

'-ink' rhyme family; others include:
ink
think
link
rink
sink
stink
wink

rhyming couplets

full of flavour, soft and sweet

alliteration

early evening light, between sunset and dark

repetition, surprise in changed structure of last 2 lines, because 'orange' is difficult to rhyme!

**R W11:** to make collections of personal interest or significant words and words linked to particular topics

**R T3:** to re-read a text to provide context cues to help read unfamiliar words

**R T10:** to re-read and recite stories and rhymes with predictable and repeated patterns and experiment with similar rhyming patterns

# Old Macdonald had a farm

## Background

This is a familiar song with a repetitive structure that makes it ideal for children to recite and extend with their own lines. The song's highly predictable pattern encourages the children to match spoken and written words, including the presentation of noise words such as *moo* and *oink*. It links with other cumulative and animal-based texts in this book – 'Cats' (page 60), 'Let's Look at Animals' (page 68), 'Down by the Cool of the Pool' (page 86) and 'Farmyard Hullabaloo' (page 88).

## Shared reading and discussing the text

● Prior to reading the text, gather together different illustrated versions of the song and other books about farm animals (see below). Display these and encourage the children to share the books and talk about the pictures. Place a play mat and models of different farm animals on the carpet.

● Ask the children if they know the song 'Old Macdonald had a farm'. Sing the song to them. Pause at each verse to allow children to find models of the animals mentioned and place them on the farm mat.

● Sing the song together, or with the children joining in with the animal noises, then make up one or two additional verses (hen – *cluck cluck*; goose – *hiss hiss*; horse – *neigh neigh* and so on).

● Highlight the words *here*, *there* and *everywhere* and use positions in the classroom to demonstrate what they mean.

## Activities

● Encourage the children to carry the song in their head. Accompany the song with hand clapping. On a specified visual signal, ask the children to stop singing but continue clapping.

Alternatively, percussion instruments can be used to beat the rhythm.

● From a range of percussion instruments, ask the children to select some to represent the animals in the song. Ask, for example, *Which instrument would be best for the cow? How should it be played?* Encourage the children to experiment and evaluate the sounds produced. In groups, help some children to recite or sing the song while others provide the percussion accompaniment.

● In guided writing, continue the composition of additional verses begun in shared reading (for example, for a donkey and cat) or use a different context for the song, for example 'Old Macdonald had a zoo', with more exotic animals, such as an elephant, lion and parrot.

● Help the children to make finger puppets of the animals. Glue two basic puppet shapes together for the children. They can glue felt shapes onto the puppets to make the features or use marker pens to draw faces. Group the children so that all those with pig puppets, for example, are sitting together. Sing the song as a class, with the groups of children singing the verse about their chosen animal.

## Extension/further reading

Help the children to practise singing the rhyme in order to perform it to other children, ideally with the percussion accompaniment.

Colin and Jacqui Hawkins (Egmont) and Siobhan Dodds (Walker Books) have produced good versions of the rhyme. Other suggestions for farm reading are Siân Phillips' readings of *Farmyard Stories for Under Fives* (Ladybird Books Audio), Eric Hill's *Spot Goes to the Farm* (Picture Puffins) and *Spot at the Farm* (Frederick Warne), and *My First Farm Board Book* (Dorling Kindersley).

R **W5:** to read on sight a range of familiar words, e.g. children's names, captions, labels, and words from favourite books

R **W11:** to make collections of personal interest or significant words and words linked to particular topics

well-known traditional song

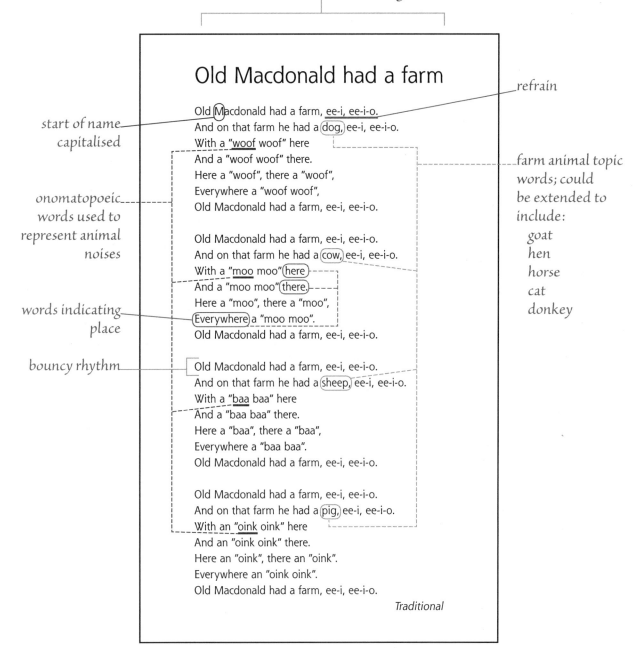

# Old Macdonald had a farm

start of name capitalised

refrain

onomatopoeic words used to represent animal noises

words indicating place

bouncy rhythm

farm animal topic words; could be extended to include:
goat
hen
horse
cat
donkey

Old Macdonald had a farm, ee-i, ee-i-o.
And on that farm he had a dog, ee-i, ee-i-o.
With a "woof woof" here
And a "woof woof" there.
Here a "woof", there a "woof",
Everywhere a "woof woof",
Old Macdonald had a farm, ee-i, ee-i-o.

Old Macdonald had a farm, ee-i, ee-i-o.
And on that farm he had a cow, ee-i, ee-i-o.
With a "moo moo" here
And a "moo moo" there.
Here a "moo", there a "moo",
Everywhere a "moo moo".
Old Macdonald had a farm, ee-i, ee-i-o.

Old Macdonald had a farm, ee-i, ee-i-o.
And on that farm he had a sheep, ee-i, ee-i-o.
With a "baa baa" here
And a "baa baa" there.
Here a "baa", there a "baa",
Everywhere a "baa baa".
Old Macdonald had a farm, ee-i, ee-i-o.

Old Macdonald had a farm, ee-i, ee-i-o.
And on that farm he had a pig, ee-i, ee-i-o.
With an "oink oink" here
And an "oink oink" there.
Here an "oink", there an "oink".
Everywhere an "oink oink".
Old Macdonald had a farm, ee-i, ee-i-o.

*Traditional*

R **T8:** to locate and read significant parts of the text, e.g. names of key characters, rhymes and chants

R **T10:** to re-read and recite stories and rhymes with predictable and repeated patterns and experiment with similar rhyming patterns

R **T14:** to use experience of poems as a basis for independent writing, e.g. retelling, substitution, extension, and through shared composition with adults

# Signs that help us

## Background

This text collects a number of different signs that children might come across during their everyday lives. Looking at signs in the local environment lets children develop their understanding of the conventions of print in different contexts, and gives context and purpose to their own writing. They will also develop their alphabetic knowledge, particularly the recognition and use of upper-case letters.

## Shared reading and discussing the text

● Arrange pictures of street furniture and direction and distance signs to create an initial stimulus display.

● Before reading the text, point to the letters on an alphabet frieze as you recite the alphabet together. Re-read the alphabet and draw attention to the differences between the capital and lower-case letters. Are some capital letters the same shape as their lower-case versions? Are some different? Ask a few children to find specific capital letters. Can they find the capital letters that begin their own names?

● Brainstorm some names of local roads and the roads where the children live. Write them on the board. Discuss how we know what the roads are called. (Names on signs at the ends of the streets.) Ask the children to think of other street notices and signs they know, for example *STOP, SCHOOL*. Add these to the board and help the children to see that the words are all in capital letters. Explain that this is so the signs are easily noticed and understood.

● Look at the signs on the text. Point out the different shapes and sizes of sign and the type used. Notice that all the signs are telling us to do something or giving us advice; they are there to help us. Which signs do the children recognise? Where have they seen them? Reinforce the use of capital letters.

● Some signs have text and some do not. Ask the children how we know what the signs without writing mean. (We can usually work it out from the picture and the context in which the sign is placed.)

## Activities

● Copy a classroom notice written in lower-case onto a large sheet of paper or interactive whiteboard, for example *turn off the light*. Model rewriting the words in capital letters. If using an interactive whiteboard, consider appropriate fonts, sizes and colours. Provide another example, such as *turn off the taps*, and ask the children to rewrite the notice a word at a time using capital letters. Let them refer to the frieze or alphabet books if they need to. You could also ask them to rewrite the signs on the text in lower-case letters.

● Arrange a walk around the local environment to find examples of signs. Decide the route you will take and arrange for additional adult help. Take photographs with a digital camera. Back in the classroom, discuss the shapes and colours of street signs and consider where they are sited. (Where they are easily visible.)

● Using the computer, children can make signs based on the street signs they found and those on the text. Encourage them to experiment with different fonts and colours. Remind them to consider what each sign is for and discuss which colours and sizes are most effective from long distances and when it is dark. Small versions can be made for use with a set of toy cars and a play mat.

● A similar activity would be to make signs for well-known stories. For instance, for 'Jack and the Beanstalk': *NO GIANTS ALLOWED!* or, on the door of the giant's castle, *BEWARE OF THE GIANT!* A sign on the troll's bridge might read *NO CROSSING FOR BILLY GOATS*. A book of the children's signs could be produced and used in shared reading.

● Help the children to make signs for use in the classroom.

● Ask the children to sort the photographs taken on the walk into those with writing and those without and add them to the display.

## Extension/further reading

Further reading might include *Shut the Gate* by Sonia Devons and Shoo Rayner (Puffin).

**R W3:** alphabetic and phonic knowledge through:
● sounding and naming each letter of the alphabet in lower and upper case
● understanding alphabetical order through alphabet books, rhymes, and songs

**R S4:** to use a capital letter for the start of own name

# Signs that help us

capital letters throughout so words are bold and stand out

tells us what to do

signs without words; pictures tell us what they mean

gives advice or information

exclamation mark

**RT1:** through shared reading:
● to recognise printed and handwritten words in a variety of settings, e.g. labels, signs, notices, directions
● that words can be written down to be read again for a wide range of purposes

**R T11:** through shared writing: to understand that writing can be used for a range of purposes, e.g. to send messages, record, inform

**R T15:** to use writing to communicate in a variety of ways, incorporating it into play and everyday classroom life, e.g. signs, directions, labels

# On the Farm

## by Henry Pluckrose

### Background

This information text uses a layout in which each sentence starts a new line, to aid accessibility. It can be a starting point for thinking about farming in the past and present and the processes that everyday commodities such as milk go through. It can be linked to other farming texts: 'Farmyard Hullabaloo' (page 88), 'Five Busy Farmers' (page 96) and 'Old Macdonald had a farm' (page 102).

### Shared reading and discussing the text

● Ask children who have visited a farm or live on a farm to share their knowledge.

● Read the text to the children. Ask some comprehension questions, for example *What are tractors used for? How often does the shepherd shear the sheep? Why does the farmer keep dairy cows?*

● Re-read the text up to *donkeys or mules* and show the children pictures of old and new farming methods. Encourage them to look carefully at the pictures as additional sources of information. What differences do they notice between old and new? Do they think farming is easier or more difficult with a tractor?

● Re-read the section on milk. Ask the children where the milk they put on their cereal comes from. How does it get into bottles or cartons? Talk about the different stages milk goes through before arriving on the table. Explain that pasteurised milk has been treated so that it doesn't contain any germs that might harm us.

● Re-read the section about sheep farming. If possible, show some untreated wool and wool products (a jumper, blanket and so on). Talk about the processes that wool goes through before it can be used in textiles. Explain that the sheep's winter coat is sheared in spring and a new one grows by the following winter.

### Activities

● Play a game of 'Where does it come from?'. Produce a simple set of cards showing food and clothing items and another set showing the original source, for example jumper, sheep; milk, cow; bread, wheat. Ask the children to match the items with their sources. Encourage them to talk about processes that different things go through before we can use them.

● Focus on sequencing. Produce a set of cards showing the sequence that milk goes through before we buy it in cartons, for example cow eating grass, cow being milked, milk being transported in a lorry, cartons on the supermarket shelf. More stages can be inserted if appropriate (pasteurisation, for example). Ask the children to refer to the text and put the cards in the correct sequence. Encourage them to talk about the process. Help more confident children to label/caption the cards. Alternatively, rather than simply placing the cards in order, children could place the pictures in position on a prepared sequence diagram with arrows.

● Talk about the different tasks that a farmer uses a tractor for. Ask the children to paint a tractor doing one of the jobs. Make a display, using a title from the text: *A tractor is a very useful machine.*

● Make a class book about farm machines. Ask the children what machines are used on a farm. List their suggestions and choose one to write about in shared writing. Ask what they already know about this piece of equipment, then list things they would like to find out. Use a range of sources to find answers to the questions. Ask the children to continue the book in guided groups. (If you have been on a farm visit, include photographs of the farm machinery. Help the children to compile a contents page and make a decorative cover for the book.) If possible, share the work with another class.

### Extension/further reading

If possible, visit a farm and write a class recount of the visit. Take digital photographs.

Investigate how wool is treated before it can be used to make clothes.

Books on farm machinery include *On the Farm* by Philip Ardagh and Tig Sutton (Belitha Press), *Tractors* by Graham Rickard (Puffin) and *Tractors and Trucks* by Robert Crowther (Walker Books).

sentences begin with capital letter and end with full stop

new line for each sentence

# On the Farm

introductory section then 3 sections, each about a different aspect of farming:

Farmers grow food.
They also care for the animals that give us meat, milk and wool.

Farmers use many different machines on the farm.
A tractor is a very useful machine.
The farmer uses the tractor to push and pull other machines.
Before tractors were invented farmers used oxen, horses, donkeys or mules.

machinery

such as plough, planter (seed drill), equipment to chop, fertilise, cultivate

created, made for the first time

dairy farming

A dairy farmer keeps cows for their milk.
The cows are milked by machine.
The milk is loaded onto a lorry and taken away.

work animal, cross breed – part horse, part donkey

have their milk extracted

sheep farming

Some farmers keep sheep.
Sheep give us meat and wool.
Each sheep is sheared once a year.
The shepherd shears the sheep with electric clippers

main focus of farm is to produce milk for dairy products: those made from cows' milk, such as cream, butter, cheese, yogurt

someone who looks after sheep

cutting tool

has its fleece removed (to make wool)

**R W7:** to read on sight the words from texts of appropriate difficulty

**R W10:** new words from their reading and shared experiences

**R T11:** through shared writing: to understand that writing can be used for a range of purposes, e.g. to record, inform

# Take a Walk on a Rainbow

by Miriam Moss

### Background

This extract is from a non-fiction book sub-titled *A first look at colour.* The concepts may be a little difficult to grasp, but the vocabulary is straightforward. The text introduces a number of colour themes, including light and dark, colour in the natural world, colours in the rainbow, colour and sight. It provides a starting point for further science explorations and can be linked to other colour texts in this book: 'One is a lion' (page 98) and 'What is pink?' (page 100).

### Shared reading and discussing the text

● Gather a selection of different-coloured fruit. If possible, have some fruit at different stages of ripeness, such as green and red tomatoes.

● Ask the children if they have ever noticed what happens to colours at night-time. (Everything seems black and grey [because there is little light].) Ask them if they have ever seen a rainbow and to describe it if they can.

● Read the text, discussing each of the facts in turn. For example, *When there's no light there's no colour: imagine going into a dark room – what do you see? What happens when you turn the light on?*

● Have a look at the fruit and consider how the colour changes as the fruit ripens. Encourage the children to relate this observation to personal experiences.

● Think aloud, *I wonder how we know that cats, dogs and horses only see in black and white?* Ask how we could find out more about this fact. Demonstrate using an encyclopedia.

● Re-read the text, encouraging the children to say familiar words with you, such as *cats, dogs, black, white, grey.*

### Activities

● Make some bubble mixture of three parts water to one part washing-up liquid. Let the children blow some bubbles (wands can be made from twisted garden wire) and encourage them to observe the 'rainbows' and reflections that appear on the bubbles' surface. Ask the children to think of words to describe bubbles (*see-through, light, floaty*), and write them down for them. Read the list of words and use them to write a list poem in shared writing.

● In shared/group work, write an account of the bubble blowing activity, breaking the procedure down into steps and emphasising the importance of writing the procedure in the correct sequence.

● Make a rainbow display: produce a large rainbow for the wall and label each of the colours with the children. Ask them to help you choose words from the text to caption the display: *The sun shines through raindrops in the air making sunlight spread out into all the colours of the rainbow.* Teach a mnemonic for remembering the order of the colours, for example *Richard Of York Gave Battle In Vain.* Place a table in front of the rainbow and use it to display different-coloured items each week. Use this colour table to refine children's description of colours, for example finding words to describe a specific shade of red (such as *pillar-box red*). Extend the children's ideas about colour. For example, include red leaves in the red display to challenge the idea that leaves are always green.

● Provide a selection of cut and uncut fruit for the children to draw. Talk about the different colours, such as the different shades of green of a kiwi fruit and the black seeds. Display the children's artwork with words from the text, for example *We can see many colours.*

### Extension/further reading

Retell stories from various cultures that give different perspectives on the origin of the rainbow, such as the Greek story of Iris, or the Norse myth of the rainbow bridge Bifrost. Sources of such tales can be found on the Internet as well as in folklore collections.

Some non-fiction books are *Colours* by Arianne Holden (Lorenz Books) and *Light and Colour* in the Evans Brothers *Young Scientists Investigate* series. A fiction suggestion is *Draw Me a Star* by Eric Carle (Puffin).

**R W2:** knowledge of grapheme/phoneme correspondences through: hearing and identifying initial sounds in words

**R W6:** to read on sight the 45 high-frequency words to be taught by the end of YR from Appendix List 1

# TAKE A WALK ON A RAINBOW

series of facts ---

Storm clouds gather and the sky turns black. When there's no light there's no colour.

Sunlight looks white but it's really made up of all the colours of the rainbow.

fact explained

apostrophe for informal contraction: 'there is'; 'it is'

words within words: 'rain', 'bow'; 'rain', 'drops'; 'sun', 'light'; 'every', 'thing'

The sun shines through raindrops in the air making sunlight spread out into all the colours of the rainbow.

not all

Some fruit changes colour when it's ripe.

ready to eat

high-frequency words

Birds can see many colours. Cats dogs and horses only see in black, white and grey.

shades

Every night the sun goes down, light fades and everything looks black and grey again.

**R T11:** through shared writing:
● to understand that writing can be used for a range of purposes, e.g. to inform, tell stories
● to apply knowledge of letter/sound correspondences in helping the teacher to scribe, and re-reading what the class has written

# The three little pigs    *Extract 1*

Once upon a time, three little pigs lived with their mother in a cottage at the edge of the woods.

One day their mother told them, "It is time for you to leave home and make your own way in the world."

So, off they went.

"Take care," Mother called as she waved goodbye, "and beware of the big bad wolf."

The first little pig built a house of straw. It didn't take her very long. Then she went out to play.

The second little pig built a house of sticks. It didn't take her very long either. Then she went out to play.

The third little pig worked very hard all day and built a house made with bricks. It was a good, strong house.

Later, the big bad wolf came out of the woods and crept up to the house made of straw.

He knocked at the door. RATATATTAT!

"Little pig, little pig, may I come in?"

"No! No!" By the hairs on my chinny chin chin I will not let you in!" the first little pig replied.

"Then I'll huff and I'll puff and I'll blow your house down!"

So the wolf huffed and puffed and blew the straw house down.

The little pig jumped up and ran to the house of sticks.

*Retold by Nikki Gamble*

# The three little pigs   *Extract 2*

The big bad wolf followed her and crept up to the house made of sticks.

He knocked at the door. RATATATTAT!

"Little pig, little pig, may I come in?"

"No! No! By the hairs on my chinny chin chin I will not let you in!" the second little pig replied.

"Then I'll huff and I'll puff and I'll blow your house down!"

So the wolf huffed and puffed and blew the stick house down.

The little pigs jumped up and ran to the house of bricks.

The big bad wolf followed them and crept up to the house.

He knocked at the door. RATATATTAT!

"Little pig, little pig, may I come in?"

"No! No! By the hairs on my chinny chin chin I will not let you in!" the third little pig replied.

"Then I'll huff and I'll puff and I'll blow your house down!"

So the wolf huffed and puffed, and he HUFFED and he PUFFED…

…but he COULD NOT blow that house down.

The wolf was VERY CROSS. "I'm coming to get you!" he shouted as he climbed onto the roof. The little pigs could hear him climbing into the chimney. Quick as a wink, the third little pig put a pot of boiling water into the fireplace. The wolf fell down the chimney straight into the pot…

…and that was the end of him!

The three little pigs lived happily ever after in the good strong house made of bricks.

*Retold by Nikki Gamble*

Term 1: Traditional stories with predictable structures and patterned language

# In the dark, dark town

In the dark, dark town,
There is a dark, dark street.

In the dark, dark street,
There is a dark, dark house.

And in the dark, dark house,
There is a dark, dark hall.

And in the dark, dark hall,
There are some dark, dark stairs.

Up the dark, dark stairs,
There is a dark, dark door.

Through the dark, dark door,
There is a dark, dark room.

In that dark, dark room,
There is a dark, dark corner.

And in the dark, dark corner,
There is a dark, dark cupboard.

And in the dark, dark cupboard,
There is…

Traditional

**SCHOLASTIC** Photocopiable

**50 Shared texts ● Year R**

# Grumble-Rumble!

*Extract 1*

Little Roo didn't want her breakfast. She didn't want her kangaflakes, or her honey on toast. She wanted to go out to play. She bounced all around the garden with her new ball.

Suddenly she heard a great big

GRUMBLE-RUMBLE!

"A monster!" cried Little Roo, and bounced off to tell her friend Crocodile.

"There's a monster following me!" cried Little Roo.

But Crocodile didn't answer. He was busy eating grapes. So Little Roo bounced off to tell Snake.

*Extract 2*

"Mummy! Mummy! There's a horrible monster following me!" cried Little Roo. And sure enough there was the **loudest**

GRUMBLE-RUMBLE! ever.

"That's not a horrible monster!" laughed Mummy Roo. "That's your hungry tummy! Would you like your kangaflakes now?"

"Yes please!" said Little Roo.

And she ate them ALL up!

*Siobhan Dodds*

# I Like Me!

This morning I stood up and said:
>I like myself from toes to head!
>I like the way I look today!
>I like the way I work and play!
>I like the way I act with friends!
>I like the way my body bends!
>I like who I was born to be!
>I like myself!
>>Hey!
>>>I like ME!

*Babs Bell Hajdusiewicz*

# PAINTING

There's red paint on my hands,

*(Wipe hands together.)*

and green paint in my hair.

*(Stroke hair with both hands.)*

There's blue paint on my nose,

*(Touch nose.)*

but I don't really care!

There's black paint on my shirt,

*(Wipe hands down front.)*

and yellow on my shoes.

*(Touch shoes.)*

There's so much paint on me,

*(Point to self.)*

there's no more paint to use!

*Linda Hammond*

# Goldilocks and the three bears

*Chorus:*

When Goldilocks went to the house of the bears

Oh, what did her blue eyes see?

1. A bowl that was huge and a bowl that was small,
   And a bowl that was tiny and that was all,
   And she counted them – one, two, three.

*Chorus*

2. A chair that was huge and a chair that was small,
   And a chair that was tiny and that was all,
   And she counted them – one, two, three.

*Chorus*

3. A bed that was huge and a bed that was small,
   And a bed that was tiny and that was all,
   And she counted them – one, two, three.

*Chorus*

4. A bear that was huge and a bear that was small,
   And a bear that was tiny and that was all,
   And they growled at her – ROARR! ROARR! ROARR!

Carolyn Sherwin Bailey

# Sounds Good

Sausage sizzles,
crispbreads crack;
hot dogs hiss
and flapjacks snap!

Bacon boils
and fritters fry;
apples squelch
in apple pie.

Baked beans bubble,
gravy grumbles;
popcorn pops,
and stomach rumbles…

**I'M HUNGRY!**


*Judith Nicholls*

# Bedtime

Five minutes, five minutes more, please!
    Let me stay five minutes more!
Can't I just finish the castle
    I'm building here on the floor?
Can't I just finish the story
    I'm reading here in my book?
Can't I just finish this bead-chain —
    It's *almost* finished, look!
Can't I just finish this game, please?
    When a game's once begun
It's a pity never to find out
    Whether you've lost or won.
Can't I stay five minutes?
    Well, can't I stay just four?
Three minutes, then? two minutes?
    Can't I stay *one* minute more?


*Eleanor Farjeon*

# My Bed

My bed is like a little boat
floating out to sea.
And now it's like an island
with a coconut tree.

My bed is like a racing car
roaring in a race.
And now it's like a rocket
rising into space.

My bed is like a submarine
diving down deep.
But now my bed is just a bed
Because I'm fast asleep.

*Tony Mitton*

**PARTY INVITATION**

Jatinder is invited to
Jack's 5th birthday party

at: Pizza Place
High Street
Smalltown

on: Saturday 19 November

time: 3.00–4.30pm

RSVP
Mrs Smith (Jack's Mum)
Tel: 011234 345678

# Menu

## Hot meals

Tomato soup ............................................. £1.00
Chicken nuggets, chips and peas .......... £3.99
Mini sausages, chips and beans............. £3.99
Cheese and tomato pizza with salad ..... £3.99
Spaghetti Bolognese............................... £3.99
Jacket potato with cheese ...................... £2.50

## Cold meals

Ham salad ................................................ £3.50
Cheese salad ........................................... £3.50
Tuna sandwich ........................................ £2.50

## Desserts

Jelly and ice cream ................................. 99p
Chocolate cake ....................................... £1.99
Selection of fruit..................................... 50p

## Drinks

Fizzy orange .......................................... small 50p
                                                    large 80p
Blackcurrant .......................................... small 50p
                                                    large 80p

*FREE lollipop for every clean plate!*

Nikki Gamble

# COOKING RULES

1. Wash your hands.

2. Wear an apron to protect your clothes.

3. Read the recipe carefully before you begin.

4. Check that you have the ingredients and equipment you need.

5. Measure out the ingredients carefully.

6. Use a separate spoon if you want to taste the mixture.

7. Ask an adult to help if you need to use the cooker or sharp knives.

8. Wear oven gloves if you are putting something in the oven or taking it out.

9. Make sure saucepan handles are safely turned to the side.

10. When you have finished cooking, remember the washing up!

Nikki Gamble

# Chocolate apples

### Get ready

2 eating apples

1 block chocolate cake covering

Sweets

Heatproof bowl

Small saucepan

Wooden skewers

Silver foil

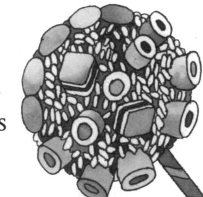

### ...Get set

Break up the chocolate into pieces.

Put it in the bowl over a pan of water.

 Slowly heat the water so the chocolate melts.

Remove the pan from the heat.

## Go!

Push the skewers into the apples.

Dip them into the melted chocolate.

Leave them to harden slightly on the foil.

Decorate with sweets.

Judy Bastyra

# LET'S LOOK AT
# Fruit

## Orange

Oranges have thick peel and tangy, juicy insides.
Oranges grow on orange trees.

## Banana

Ripe bananas are soft and squashy.
Bananas grow on tall banana palms.

## Pineapple

Pineapples have prickly, tough skins and crisp, yellow flesh.
Pineapples grow at the top of a pineapple plant.

## Mango

Mangoes have juicy yellow flesh and a big stone in the middle.
Mangoes grow on long stalks on mango trees.

Taken from LET'S Look at Fruit, published by Lorenz Books

**SCHOLASTIC** **Photocopiable**                    **50 Shared texts ● Year R**

# My body

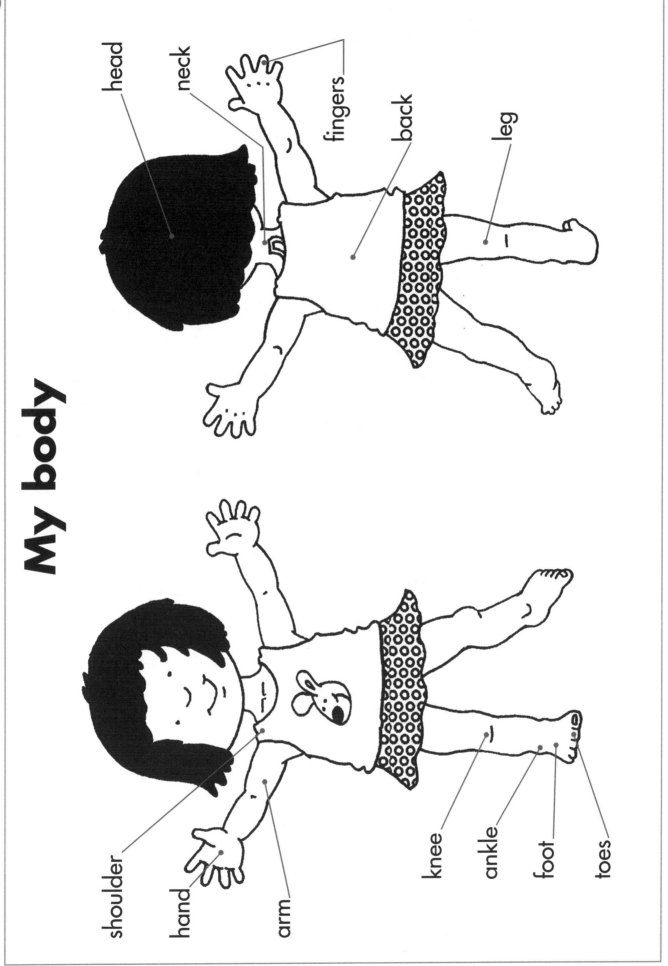

# WET WORLD

*Extract 1*

I walk on the wet world
Wet mud tugs my boots
Wet pavement splashes my boots
Wet rain sprinkles my hat
Wet rain drips down my coat

Wet cars swish down my road
Windscreen wipers wipe the wet

Whish      whish
whish      whish
Whish away the wet

*Extract 2*

Wet puddles cover wet boots
Dry feet in wet boots
Dry arms in wet coat
Dry head in wet hat
Dry me

Wet world

Norma Simon

# A Summery Saturday Morning

We take the dogs down the wiggly track,
The wiggly track, the wiggly track.
One dog's white and the other dog's black
On a summery Saturday morning.

A goose looks out of the tangled green,
The tangled green, the tangled green.
Her neck is long and her eye is mean
On a summery Saturday morning.

Another goose… and then another,
Then another, then another!
Seven sleek sisters out with mother
On a summery Saturday morning.

The geese begin to run away,
Run away, run away.
The dogs run, too. They want to play
On a summery Saturday morning.

We run, too, to catch the dogs,
To catch the dogs, to catch the dogs –
Scattering shells and leaping logs
On a summery Saturday morning.

The geese turn round and flap and hiss,
Flap and hiss, flap and hiss.
The dogs were not expecting this
On a summery Saturday morning.

The geese begin to chase us back,
To chase us back, to chase us back.
Out of the mud and up the track
On a summery Saturday morning.

*If* you want to walk in peace,
Walk in peace, walk in peace,
Don't let your dogs upset the geese
On a summery Saturday morning.

*Margaret Mahy*

Term 2: Stories with predictable structures and patterned language; number stories

# Five Ducks Five

Five ducks five began to dive.
Mr Fox came closer.
One duck swam away,
down to the rickety bridge.

Four ducks four reached the shore.
Mr Fox came closer and closer.
One duck flew away,
down to the rickety bridge.

Three ducks three flew into a tree.
Mr Fox came closer and closer.
One duck flew away,
down to the rickety bridge.

Two ducks two had things to do.
Mr Fox came even closer.
One duck crept away,
to the end of the rickety bridge.

One duck one sat in the sun,
all alone on the rickety bridge.
Mr Fox came right up close and …

# Mr Fox pounced!

The rickety bridge broke and

# SPLASH!

Mr Fox fell into the river.

*Sarah Hayes*

# Wolf's diary

# July

## Monday 1

I called on the little pigs. They did not want to play. So I huffed and I puffed, but I could not blow their house down. I came home without any tea! BOO! HOO!

## Tuesday 2

Little Red Riding Hood and her grandmother came for tea. We had toast, strawberry jam and cakes. YUM! YUM!

## Wednesday 3

A lovely sunny day. I played in the garden with the Seven Little Kids. At teatime we had lemonade and strawberries and cream. DELICIOUS!

## Thursday 4

Went to the park with Red Riding Hood. We played on the swings and slides all afternoon. I had an iced lolly from the ice-cream van. SCRUMPTIOUS!

## Friday 5

Watched 'Wolf Tales', my favourite TV programme. Had hot, buttered crumpets for tea. MOUTH-WATERING!

## Saturday 6

Went to see my favourite football team, Wolves. They're the greatest! At half time I bought a burger. TASTY!

## Sunday 7

The three little pigs invited me to their birthday party. I gave them a present. Then we ate chocolate birthday cake. SCRUMMY YUMMY!

Nikki Gamble

# I hear thunder

I hear thunder,

I hear thunder,

Oh! don't you?

Oh! don't you?

Pitter, patter raindrops.

Pitter, patter raindrops.

I'm wet through.

I'm wet through


I see blue skies.

I see blue skies.

Way up high.

Way up high.

Hurry up the sunshine.

Hurry up the sunshine.

I'll soon dry.

I'll soon dry.

*Traditional*

# I Do Not Mind You, Winter Wind

I do not mind you, Winter Wind
when you come whirling by,
to tickle me with snowflakes
drifting softly from the sky.

I do not even mind you
when you nibble at my skin,
scrambling over all of me
attempting to get in.

But when you bowl me over
and I land on my behind,
then I must tell you, Winter Wind,
I mind… I really mind!

*Jack Prelutsky*

# The Bad Day ABC

A    An alien ate my alarm clock.

B    A bear in the bathroom bawled, "Boo!"

C    A crocodile crunched up my cornflakes.

D    A dragon drawled, "How do you do?"

E    An elephant said, "Eggs are easy!"

F    A fox found my football was flat.

G    A gorilla got into my go-kart.

H    A hippo hip-hopped on my hat.

Hilda Offen

# A Week at Gran's

On Monday we went to the seaside
And I had a donkey-ride.

On Tuesday it rained all day.
We sat and played games inside.

On Wednesday we went to a fair
And I won a doll on a string.

On Thursday we went to the shops
Gran bought me this pretty ring.

On Friday we packed a picnic
And paddled in the pool in the park.

On Saturday we had a barbecue
And stayed up till it got dark.

On Sunday we packed our cases.
And Dad came in the afternoon.

As we waved goodbye, I shouted,
"Please can we come back soon!"

*John Foster*

# Monsters

Five purple monsters
went out to explore.
One fell down a hole,
so that left four.

Four purple monsters
went down to the sea.
One swam far away,
so that left three.

Three purple monsters
went out to the zoo.
One joined the lions,
so that left two.

Two purple monsters
went out in the sun.
One got far too hot,
so that left one.

One purple monster
went out to have fun.
Lost his way going home,
so that left none.

*Linda Hammond*

# CATS

Cats sleep
Anywhere,
Any table,
Any chair,
Top of piano,
Window-ledge
In the middle,
On the edge,
Open drawer,
Empty shoe,
Anybody's
Lap will do,
Fitted in a
Cardboard box,
In the cupboard
With your frocks –
Anywhere!
*They* don't care!
Cats sleep
Anywhere.

*Eleanor Farjeon*

# What's in the Box?

What's in the toy box?
What's in the box?
What's in the box
With the big brass locks?

There's a one-eyed ted
And a ball that's red,
Some building bricks
And a clock that ticks,
A plastic boat
And a duck that floats,
A wind-up car
And a silver star,
A doll that cries
And a plane that flies.

That's what's in the toy box!
That's what's in the box!

*Trevor Millum*

# THE APPLE AND THE WORM

I bit an apple
    That had a worm.
I swallowed the apple,
    I swallowed the worm.
I felt it squiggle,
    I felt it squirm.
I felt it wiggle,
    I felt it turn.
I felt it so slippery,
    Slimy, scummy,
I felt it land – PLOP –
    In my tummy!

I guess that worm is there to stay
Unless…
I swallow a bird some day!

*Robert Heidbreder*

# Here is the Seed

Here is the seed,
Small and round,
Hidden underneath
The ground.

Here is the shoot,
Tiny and small,
Slowly, slowly
Growing tall.

Here is the sun.
Here is the shower.
Here are the petals.
Here is the flower.

John Foster

# LET'S LOOK AT
# Animals

## Rabbit

Rabbits have twitchy noses and long ears. They hop along the ground. When baby rabbits are born, they live in a soft, warm nest with their mother. Some rabbits are kept as pets, others live wild in the countryside. Have you ever seen a wild rabbit?

## Duck

A duck can walk on land, fly in the air, and swim in ponds and rivers.
Ducks like to live near water.
Do any ducks live near you?
Ducks dive down to find tiny creatures to eat in the wet mud.
A baby duck is called a duckling.

Taken from Let's Look at Animals by Nicola Tuxworth, published by Lorenz Books

# WHY

## DO SUNFLOWERS FACE THE SUN?

### Why do sunflowers turn towards the sun?

Sunflowers' beautiful, yellow heads and green leaves follow the sun across the sky, making warm landing pads for bees and catching lots of energy-giving light.

### Why do plants have to be watered?

Next time it rains, think about the plants outside. They use rainwater to make food and to hold up their leaves. Indoor plants would die if we didn't give their thirsty roots a drink.

### Why do cactuses have prickles?

Cactuses are the roughest, toughest plants in the desert. Their sharp prickles protect them from hungry animals and collect precious water from dewdrops.

*Terry Martin*

*Thompson & Morgan*

# CHILDREN'S COLLECTION

## HOW TO GROW CRESS

Put 4 or 5 layers of kitchen paper on to a saucer and pour on a little water. Sprinkle a thick layer of seed over the paper. Put your saucer into a clear bag and seal. Place in a dark cupboard. Check your seeds regularly. When they grow to 1cm, place on a windowsill. Grow your cress for another week or so until you are ready to eat. Cut the leaves off just above the paper. Cress is tasty in salads as well as in sandwiches.

PACKET CONTENTS: One packet of each of the following: Cress, Radish, Giant Sunflower and Poached Eggs.

**Thompson & Morgan (UK) Ltd**
Poplar Lane  Ipswich  England  IP8 3BU

THOMPSON & MORGAN
• Quality
Guaranteed •
LABORATORY & FIELD TESTED

In the unlikely event you have any cause to complain, please return this packet for credit or replacement.

# Weather map

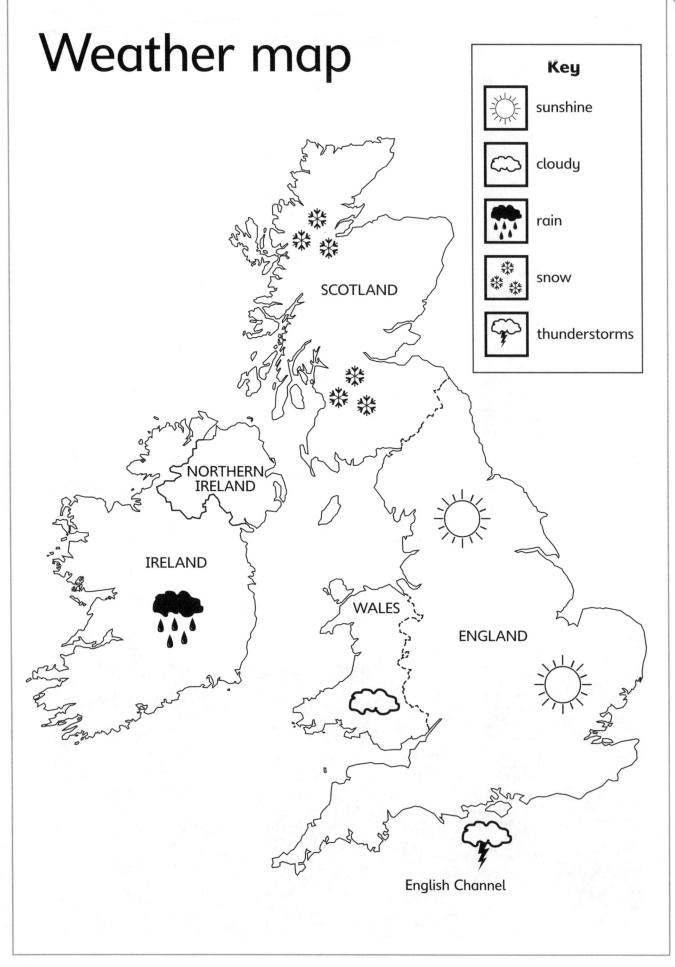

**Key**

| | |
|---|---|
| ☀ | sunshine |
| ☁ | cloudy |
| 🌧 | rain |
| ❄ | snow |
| ⛈ | thunderstorms |

SCOTLAND

NORTHERN IRELAND

IRELAND

WALES

ENGLAND

English Channel

# The Three Billy Goats Gruff

*Extract 1*

Once, by the bank of a river, there lived three Billy Goats Gruff. They were very happy for they had all the grass they could eat. But one day the smallest Billy Goat Gruff said to his brothers, "Let's cross the river; the grass looks much greener and sweeter on the other side."

His brothers agreed that the grass did look greener and sweeter, and they decided to cross the little wooden bridge over the river, one at a time.

But a fierce troll lived under the bridge.

When the little goat clattered across the bridge, the fierce troll jumped up and growled in his scariest voice, "Who's that trip-trapping over my bridge?"

"It is only me," said the little billy goat.

"I'M GOING TO EAT YOU UP!"

"If you let me pass, my bigger brother will cross the bridge, and he is much larger and juicier than me," said the little goat.

"Very well," said the troll, and he let the little goat go over the bridge.

*Retold by Nikki Gamble*

# The Three Billy Goats Gruff

*Extract 2*

Next came the middle Billy Goat Gruff. As he clattered across the bridge, the fierce troll jumped up and growled in his scariest voice, "Who's that trip-trapping over my bridge?"

"It is only me," said the middle billy goat.

"I'M GOING TO EAT YOU UP!"

If you let me pass, my bigger brother will cross the bridge, and he is much larger and juicier than me," said the middle-sized goat.

"Well, alright," said the troll, who was getting very hungry indeed, and he let the middle-sized goat go over the bridge.

Last of all came the oldest and biggest Billy Goat Gruff. As he clattered loudly onto the bridge, the fierce troll jumped up and growled in his scariest voice, "Who's that trip-trapping over my bridge?"

"ME!" roared the biggest billy goat. He charged across the bridge and butted the troll headlong into the river. The troll was swept away and nobody ever heard of him again.

But the Billy Goats Gruff lived for a long time and enjoyed the sweet, delicious grass on the other side of the river.

*Retold by Nikki Gamble*

# CHICKEN LICKEN

*Extract 1*

ONE DAY, WHEN Chicken Licken was in the wood, an acorn fell from a tree on to his poor bald head.

"Oh dear," thought Chicken Licken. "The sky is falling! I must go and tell the king."

So he left the wood and headed for the king's palace. On the way there he met Hen Len.

"Well, Hen Len," he said, "where are you going?"

"I'm going to the wood," said Hen Len.

"Oh, don't go there," said Chicken Licken, "for I was there and the sky fell on my poor bald head and I'm going to tell the king."

"Can I come with you?" asked Hen Len.

"Certainly," said Chicken Licken. So they both went off together to tell the king the sky was falling.

As they travelled along, they met Cock Lock. "Well, Cock Lock," said Hen Len, "where are you going?"

"I'm going to the wood," said Cock Lock.

"Oh, Cock Lock, don't go there, said Hen Len, "for Chicken Licken was there and the sky fell on his poor bald head and we're going to tell the king."

"May I come with you?" said Cock Lock.

"Certainly," said Chicken Licken.

So off they all went together to tell the king the sky was falling.

# CHICKEN LICKEN

*Extract 2*

A little while later they met Fox Lox. And Fox Lox said, "Where are you going?"

"Chicken Licken was in the wood and the sky fell on his poor bald head," said all the birds together, "and we're going to tell the king."

"Come with me," said Fox Lox, "and I will show you the way to the palace. The king will be delighted to see you."

They all followed Fox Lox until they came to a dark, dark hole in the edge of the hillside. "This is the way to the king's palace," said Fox Lox. So in went Chicken Licken, Hen Len, Cock Lock, Duck Luck, Drake Lake, Goose Loose and Turkey Lurkey, one after the other. But this was not the way to the king's palace, it was Fox Lox's den. And in no time at all Fox Lox had gobbled up every one of them, so they never saw the king to tell him that the sky was falling.

# What is the moon?

*Extract 1*

*What is the moon?*
It's a light in the sky that makes
the dark bright.

*Does it shine every night?*
Sometimes we can't see it
but the moon is still there.

*But where is it, where?*
It might go behind clouds,
maybe to sleep,
or to play
hide and seek.

*Will it play with me?*
We'll see, but now
it's time for your tea.

*Extract 2*

The moon is a world as big as ours
but no people are there,
it just lives with the stars.

*That sounds very sad. I'll fly up and see
if the moon would like to play with me.*
No, not right now, it's so far away,
to get there would take a year and a day.

*But look at the sky, the moon is so near.*
It seems that way, because the night is clear.

*But Mum, can't you see, it's waving to me…
I'm going right now to the moon for my tea*

Caroline Dunant

# Down by the Cool of the Pool

Down by the pool
in the cool of the day,
Frog cried, "Wheeeee!
Can you dance like me?"

Duck came to see.
"I can dance too. But not like you.
I can flap."
So Duck went "flap"
And Frog cried, "Wheeeee!
Can you dance like me?"
Down by the cool of the pool.

Pig came to see.
"I can dance too. But not like you.
I can wiggle."
So Pig went "wiggle",
Duck went "flap",
And Frog cried, "Wheeeee!
Can you dance like me?"
Down by the cool of the pool...

...Into the pool they flapped and they flopped.
But did that stop them?
No! No! No!
For they all cried, "Ooh!" and "Whooop!" and "Wheeee!"
"Come and see. Oh, ha-ha-hee!"
We're having fun, dancing our dance
**in** the cool of the pool!"

*Tony Mitton*

# FARMYARD HULLABALOO

## Extract 1

Early in the morning
As the sun begins to rise,
The pigs are feeling hungry
And they're snoring in their sties.

The rooster wakes the farm up
With a cock-a-doodle-doo!
The sheepdog won't stop barking,
And the cows begin to moo.

## Extract 2

### COW

Sometimes I moo while I'm chewing
I hope you don't think that it's rude,
But mooing and chewing
Are what I like doing.
Do you moo when you chew your food?

### PIGS

I love looking after my piglets
And watching them wriggle and squeal.
They clamber all over each other all day
To snuffle around for a meal.

### SHEEP

I've got a lovely fluffy fleece
Which makes me very proud,
So I skip around my meadow
Make-believing I'm a cloud.

## Extract 3

Now it's night time on the farmyard
And the moon is shining bright,
It's time to leave the animals
And wave them all goodnight.

Giles Andreae

# Rocket song

Boom off!
Zoom off!
Now we're on our way.
Our rocket's left the launching pad
And we're in space today.

Drop down!
Plop down!
Get the buggy out.
It's just the thing upon the moon
To help us get about.

Crash down!
Splash down!
We go back to a ship
With cheers and claps and handshakes
To end our first moon trip.

*Barbara Ireson*

# Early in the morning

Come down to the station early in the morning,
See all the railway trains standing in a row.
See all the drivers starting up the engines,
Clickety click and clickety clack,
Off they go!

Come down to the garage early in the morning,
See all the buses standing in a row.
See all the drivers starting up the engines,
Rumble, rumble, rumble, rumble,
Off they go!

Come down to the seaside early in the morning,
See all the motor-boats floating in a row.
See all the drivers starting up the engines,
Splishing, splishing, sploshing, sploshing,
Off they go!

Come down to the airport early in the morning,
See all the aeroplanes standing in a row.
See all the pilots starting up the engines,
Whirring, whirring, whirring, whirring,
Off they go!

*Barbara Ireson*

# The Train Journey

The train is running on the

track track track

And I'm sitting in the carriage at the

back back back

For we're going on a journey that is

fast fast fast

The fields and the cows whizz

past past past

We're going to the seaside very

quick quick quick

And I'm listening to the wheels as they

click click click

And we're going over the hills to the

top top top


But slowly…

very slowly…

We come to a station and we

stop…

*stop…*

*stop!*


*Brenda Williams*

# Five Busy Farmers

Five busy farmers
Wake up with the sun,
It was early morning
When chores must be done.

The first busy farmer
Went to milk the cow,
The second busy farmer
Thought he'd better plough.

The third busy farmer
Fed the hungry hens,
The fourth busy farmer
Mended broken pens.

The fifth busy farmer
Took his vegetables to town,
Baskets filled with cabbages
And sweet potatoes, brown.

When the work was finished
And the western sky was red,
Five busy farmers
Tumbled into bed.

*Traditional*

# One is a lion

One is a lion, yellow and strong,

Two is a green frog, jumping along.

Three is an elephant, grey and tall,

Four is a goldfish, orange and small.

Five is a polar bear, furry and white,

Six a pink pig, which squeals in delight!

Seven is a puppy, cuddly and black,

Eight a brown hen, on farmyard track.

Nine is a red robin, high in a tree,

Ten is a blue whale, deep in the sea.

*Brenda Williams*

# What is pink?

What is pink? a rose is pink
By the fountain's brink.
What is red? a poppy's red
In its barley bed.
What is blue? the sky is blue
Where the clouds float thro'.
What is white? a swan is white
Sailing in the light.
What is yellow? pears are yellow,
Rich and ripe and mellow.
What is green? the grass is green,
With small flowers between.
What is violet? clouds are violet
In the summer twilight.
What is orange? why, an orange,
Just an orange!

*Christina Rossetti*

# Old Macdonald had a farm

Old Macdonald had a farm, ee-i, ee-i-o.
And on that farm he had a dog, ee-i, ee-i-o.
With a "woof woof" here
And a "woof woof" there.
Here a "woof", there a "woof",
Everywhere a "woof woof",
Old Macdonald had a farm, ee-i, ee-i-o.

Old Macdonald had a farm, ee-i, ee-i-o.
And on that farm he had a cow, ee-i, ee-i-o.
With a "moo moo" here
And a "moo moo" there.
Here a "moo", there a "moo",
Everywhere a "moo moo".
Old Macdonald had a farm, ee-i, ee-i-o.

Old Macdonald had a farm, ee-i, ee-i-o.
And on that farm he had a sheep, ee-i, ee-i-o.
With a "baa baa" here
And a "baa baa" there.
Here a "baa", there a "baa",
Everywhere a "baa baa".
Old Macdonald had a farm, ee-i, ee-i-o.

Old Macdonald had a farm, ee-i, ee-i-o.
And on that farm he had a pig, ee-i, ee-i-o.
With an "oink oink" here
And an "oink oink" there.
Here an "oink", there an "oink".
Everywhere an "oink oink".
Old Macdonald had a farm, ee-i, ee-i-o.

*Traditional*

# Signs that help us

# On the Farm

Farmers grow food.
They also care for the animals
that give us meat, milk and
wool.

Farmers use many different
machines on the farm.
A tractor is a very useful
machine.
The farmer uses the tractor to
push and pull other machines.
Before tractors were invented
farmers used oxen, horses,
donkeys or mules.

A dairy farmer keeps cows for their milk.
The cows are milked by machine.
The milk is loaded onto a lorry and taken away.

Some farmers keep
sheep.
Sheep give us meat
and wool.
Each sheep is sheared once
a year.
The shepherd shears the sheep
with electric clippers.

Henry Pluckrose

# TAKE A WALK
## ON A
# RAINBOW

Storm clouds gather and the sky turns black.
When there's no light there's no colour.

Sunlight looks white but it's really made up of
all the colours of the rainbow.

The sun shines through raindrops in the
air making sunlight spread out into all the
colours of the rainbow.

Some fruit changes colour when it's ripe.

Birds can see many colours. Cats, dogs and
horses only see in black, white and grey.

Every night the sun goes down, light fades
and everything looks black and grey again.

Miriam Moss

# Acknowledgements

The publishers gratefully acknowledge permission to reproduce the following copyright material:

**The Agency** for an extract from *The Bad Day ABC* by Hilda Offen © 1996, Hilda Offen (1996, Hamish Hamilton). **Anness Publishing Ltd** for extracts from *Let's Look at Fruit* © 1996, Anness Publishing Ltd (1996, Lorenz Books) and for extracts from *Let's Look at Animals* by Nicola Tuxworth © 1996, Anness Publishing Ltd (1996, Lorenz Books). **John Foster** for 'A Week at Gran's' from *My Magic Anorak and Other Poems* by John Foster © 1999, John Foster (1999, Oxford University Press) and for 'Here is the Seed' from *Rhyme Time: Around the Year* compiled by John Foster © 2001, John Foster (2001, Oxford University Press). **Babs Bell Hajdusiewicz** for 'I Like Me!' by Babs Bell Hajdusiewicz from *My Family and Me* chosen by John Foster © 1999, Babs Bell Hajdusiewicz (1999, Oxford University Press). **HarperCollins Publishers (USA)** for 'I Do Not Mind You, Winter Wind' from *It's Snowing! It's Snowing!* by Jack Prelutsky © 1984, Jack Prelutsky (1984, Greenwillow Books). **David Higham Associates** for 'Cats' from *The Children's Bells* by Eleanor Farjeon © 1957, Eleanor Farejon (1957, Oxford University Press); for 'Bedtime' from *Blackbird Has Spoken* by Eleanor Farjeon © Eleanor Farjeon (Macmillan) and for four verses from *Down by the Cool of the Pool* by Tony Mitton and Guy Parker Rees, text © 2001, Tony Mitton illustrations © 2001, Guy Parker Rees (2001, Orchard Books). **Hodder & Stoughton Publishers** for an extract from *Take a Walk on a Rainbow* by Miriam Moss © 1999, Miriam Moss (1999, MacDonald Young Books). **Barbara Ireson** for 'Rocket song' from *Spaceman, Spaceman* by Barbara Ireson © Barbara Ireson (*Storychair* series, Transworld) and for 'Early in the morning' from *Over and Over Again* by Barbara Ireson © 1978, Barbara Ireson (1978, Beaver Books). **Trevor Millum** for 'What's in the Box?' by Trevor Millum from *A Teeny Tiny Teddy* chosen by John Foster © 1999, Trevor Millum (1999, Oxford University Press). **Tony Mitton** for 'My Bed' by Tony Mitton from *I'm Riding on a Giant* chosen by John Foster ©

1999, Tony Mitton (1999, Oxford University Press). **Judith Nicholls** for 'Sounds Good' from *Higgledy-Humbug* by Judith Nicholls © 1990, Judith Nicholls (1990, Mary Glasgow Publications). **The Penguin Group (UK)** for an extract from *Why do sunflowers face the sun?* by Terry Martin © 1996, Terry Martin (1996, Dorling Kindersley); for extracts from *Grumble-Rumble!* by Siobhan Dodds © 2000, Siobhan Dodds (2000, Dorling Kindersley); for 'Painting' and 'Monsters' from *One Blue Boat* by Linda Hammond © 1991, Linda Hammond (1991, Viking) and for an extract from *A Summery Saturday Morning* by Margaret Mahy © 1998, Margaret Mahy (1998, Hamish Hamilton). **The Random House Group** for extracts from 'What is the moon?' by Caroline Dunant from *Night Night Sleep Tight* © 1998, Caroline Dunant (1998, Bodley Head). **Thompson and Morgan (UK) Ltd** for instructions 'How to Grow Cress' from the *Children's Collection* seed packet © Thompson & Morgan (UK) Ltd. **Walker Books Ltd** for extracts from *Wet World* by Norma Simon and Alexi Natchev Text © 1995, Norma Simon (1995, Walker Books) and for an extract from *Nine Ducks Nine* by Sarah Hayes © 1990, Sarah Hayes (1990, Walker Books). **The Watts Publishing Group** for an extract from *Machines at Work: On the Farm* by Henry Pluckrose © 1998, Henry Pluckrose (1998, Franklin Watts: a division of The Watts Group) and for 'Chocolate Apples' from *Get Set Go: Fruit* by Judy Bastyra © 1994, Judy Bastyra (1994, Franklin Watts: a division of The Watts Group). **The Watts Group** for extracts from *Cock-a-doodle-doo! Farmyard Hullabaloo* by Giles Andreae © 1999, Giles Andreae (1999, Orchard Books). **Brenda Williams** for 'The Train Journey' by Brenda Williams from *Rhyme Time: Around the Year* compiled by John Foster © 2001, John Foster (2001, Oxford University Press) and for 'One is a lion' by Brenda Williams © 2004, Brenda Williams, previously unpublished.

Every effort has been made to trace copyright holders for the works reproduced in this book, and the publishers apologise for any inadvertent omissions.